History as a Tool in Critical Interpretation

History as a Tool in Critical Interpretation

A Symposium

Monroe C. Beardsley
E. H. Gombrich
Karsten Harries
E. D. Hirsch, Jr.
René Wellek

Edited by
Thomas F. Rugh and
Erin R. Silva

Brigham Young University Press

International Standard Book Number: 0-8425-1291-8
Library of Congress Catalog Card Number: 78-24729

Brigham Young University Press, Provo, Utah 84602
© 1978 by Brigham Young University Press. All rights reserved
Printed in the United States of America

78   2Mp   34712

Notes on Contributors

Monroe C. Beardsley, Temple University, is the author of *Aesthetics: Problems in the Philosophy of Criticism, Aesthetics from Classical Greece to the Present,* and numerous other books, articles, and reviews. Professor Beardsley currently serves as the book review editor for the *Journal of Aesthetics and Art Criticism.*

E. H. Gombrich, emeritus, University of London, is the author of *The Story of Art, Art and Illusion, In Search of Cultural History,* and *Meditations on a Hobby Horse* among many other books, articles, and reviews. Sir Ernst Gombrich is the recently retired director of the Warburg Institute at the University of London.

Karsten Harries, Yale University, is the author of *The Meaning of Modern Art,* many articles, several about Martin Heidegger, and numerous reviews. Professor Harries is chairman of the Department of Philosophy at Yale.

E. D. Hirsch, Jr., is the author of *Validity in Interpretation, The Aims of Interpretation,* and a variety of articles about hermeneutics. Professor Hirsch is the Kenan Professor of English at the University of Virginia.

René Wellek, emeritus, Yale University, is the author of *Concepts of Criticism, Discriminations, The History of Modern Criticism 1750–1950,* and hundreds of other books, articles, and reviews. Professor Wellek is currently working on the fifth volume of his history of criticism.

Contents

Introduction

There are certain theoretical questions in the humanities which, rather than leading critics toward a consensus, seem to move them into an expanding complexity of interpretation and analysis. One such question served as the theme for the first Brigham Young University Symposium on the Humanities: "Does history constitute a legitimate critical tool for the art or literary critic?" During two days of presentations and discussions, the question was quickly magnified into many issues spanning the humanistic disciplines of art history, English and comparative literature, and philosophy. Specific interests in each particular discipline ultimately led to questions common to the wide range of humanistic scholarship.

This volume constitutes a partial record of the conference proceedings, including papers written as responses to certain issues raised during the symposium. The concluding paper in this volume, an examination of the literary criticism of Edmund Wilson that was delivered at the symposium by René Wellek, comes from the fifth volume of his *History of Modern Criticism* (forthcoming). We thank him for allowing us to include his paper which raises, in acute form, the question of historical and social criticism.

In "On the Relevance of History to Art Criticism," Monroe Beardsley reasons toward a judicious use of history in art criticism by attempting to separate historical from ahistorical critical questions. By exploring the questions of meaning, Beardsley then draws distinctions between historical and ahistorical methods of interpretation.

E. H. Gombrich's response to the question of history as a tool in critical interpretation is framed by his definition of history: history is the record of events, and for this record to have meaning, the critic must make a selection based on interest. Each judgment that the critic chooses to make, whether the judgment is one based on originality or one based on physiognomic characteristics, is made within the framework of a historical matrix. Gombrich suggests that without such a framework art works could be enjoyed, but they could not be criticized.

However, Gombrich does not want to defend a purely historical approach; he does want to submit that history plays a part, often a crucial part, in the context of critical judgments. The determination of excellence in particular art works and the phenomena Gombrich calls "problem-solutions" illustrate history's part in criticism that is rooted in comparisons. He offers the hypothesis that art works are in themselves historical events, and that as art works are criticized and joined with the canon of art they will one day become history in a valuative sense. Thus Gombrich's proposition becomes a historical hypothesis.

Beardsley proposes some questions at issue in judging a work of art as a solution to certain "problems" that seemed to exist during a particular art historical period. "I do not deny that we can frame various restricted or guarded sorts of value judgments that essentially involve historical comparisons; I only hold out for the existence of other value judgments . . . that are, so to speak, history-free, yet intelligible and arguable." He wants to remove " 'artistic problems' from something in the actual life-world of the painter, open to historical inquiry, to an ahistorical dimension or parameter of the art of painting."

Beardsley's criticism of the historical approach is directed at the difficulties he finds in Gombrich's account of expressiveness in art. Beardsley's analysis is important, because it is Gombrich who has suggested that it may be an illusion to say that judgments about expressiveness in art are fundamentally ahistorical judgments. Beardsley does not suggest that he has disproved Gombrich's account of expression, but he does point out some areas of perplexity in Gombrich's analysis.

René Wellek deals with both aspects of the ahistorical-historical controversy. History, on the one hand, cannot be avoided. Literature, says Wellek, must be viewed against the backdrop of history so that one gains not only a greater feeling for its historical context, but so that one may also know of the work's originality, a factor Wellek considers important in the critical judgment of literature. (The question of novelty becomes an important point of dialogue between the symposium participants during the panel discussion included in this volume.)

Wellek warns, however, that too much literary history can be a dangerous thing "when it obscures the mind's aesthetic judgment, when this background information overwhelms the work of art." It is the aesthetic judgment that determines the quality of a work of art, he says, and history eventually fails in determining quality.

Like Wellek, Beardsley wants to caution against the overuse or misuse of historical information in art or literary criticism. Knowledge, he argues, is better than ignorance, yet critics must be careful not to misdirect their knowledge into what appears (falsely) to be a logically correct argument.

Wellek's most provocative point involves the problem of historicism—historical relativism—in literary criticism. With such a view comes the notion that every work of literature is relative to its time and place. This relativism requires that the critic have a sympathetic attitude toward each literary work produced. It is a dangerous view, says Wellek, because the critic is no longer a discriminator; he no longer holds an opinion. The critic is left saying, "I don't know." Wellek challenges humanists to choose, to make decisions between good and bad literature, and to defend their decisions based on certain theoretical criteria.

Unlike Beardsley, Gombrich, or Wellek, E. D. Hirsch asserts that the question of history as a tool in critical interpretation is not a strictly theoretical issue, but an ethical one with practical consequences. The arguments surrounding the question do not derive from the nature of art or literature, but from "some ethical preference about art, or about the way to interpret it. . . ." Thus Hirsch argues that imperatives that demand either a pure aesthetic or a pure historical approach may be equally ill-founded, and he suggests that to hold fast to either view may lead to embarrassing practical consequences.

To illustrate the problem of aesthetic and historical critical views, Hirsch presents a "thought experiment" involving the last four lines of Keats's "Ode on a Grecian Urn." Hirsch suggests that if, as a hypothetical example, we discovered a letter in which Keats explains what he meant in the last lines of his poem, then the theoretical issue ceases to have any practical consequences. These lines are now among the thousands of verses that everyone understands and accepts; even though the aesthetic or existential critic would argue that neither Keats nor anyone else has exclusive ownership of the poem's meaning, Hirsch says that such an argument has lost its practical effect.

From the viewpoint of philosophy and the philosopher, Karsten Harries believes history's role as a critical tool has unique practical implications for his discipline. More than a useless pastime or a harmless indulgence, philosophy deals with a fundamental question: "Where is man's place?" The relevance of history to this question is Harries's central issue. In his paper Harries presents the ahistorical position of philosophy which argues that, although historical scholarship may better help the reader of a philosophical text to understand its background and sources, such scholarship does not advance one's knowledge of philosophy. By analogy, how much better does one understand geometry by studying the history of geometry? Harries challenges this hostile relationship between historical and philosophical reflection by indicating a more important role for history in philosophy.

Harries suggests that philosophy is the gadfly of culture. But with this charge comes philosophy's often too-close familiarity with culture, which creates a distorted view that makes philosophical questions superficial and often meaningless. What makes the philosopher's questions meaningful is their historical context. Thus Harries suggests, "Only a philosophy that allies itself with history can hope to exhibit the presuppositions that determine our culture. Only in uncovering the presuppositions do we gain that distance from them which is a necessary condition of critical evaluation. . . . History sets limits to the kind of answer that can be given to the question: what is our place?"

Because man continues to be concerned about "his place," he will formulate new questions worthy of reflection and investigation. The relevance of history to criticism remains a lively scholarly question which, if carefully pursued, should lead to a better understanding of human experience.

We are indebted to many individuals for their support and encouragement from the very earliest stages of the symposium to the publication of this volume. Within the College of Humanities we wish to extend our appreciation to Bruce B. Clark, Dean of the college; Todd A. Britsch, chairman of the Department of Humanities, Classics, and Comparative Literature; and Professor Steven P. Sondrup. To all those involved in typing and editing our manuscript we extend our gratitude, particularly to Brenda.

We wish to note that the short essays in this volume: "A Historical Hypothesis," "Literary History and Literary Criticism," and "The Well-Read Urn: A Thought Experiment" were delivered as prefatory observations to the dialogue: history as a critical tool.

On the
Relevance of History
to Art Criticism

Monroe C. Beardsley

Questions of relevance, which are among the most important we ask, must be handled with care if they are not to occasion pointless and fruitless disputes. When clearly articulated, they are seen to be either causal or logical—that is, they concern the influence one event or state of affairs exerts upon another or they concern the logical support one proposition gives to another. Being a philosopher, I am naturally more interested in connections of the latter than in those of the former sort. This bent, with its consequent narrowing of focus, will be evident in the course of my essay. I discuss the bearing of history upon art criticism (whatever art may be in question) by asking: What sorts of historical information, if any, are required to justify our acceptance of particular sorts of statement made by critics?

I trust it will not be taken amiss if I forestall what may seem a very remotely possible misunderstanding by remarking that I am not concerned here with the relevance of historical information to art history. It is a truism—though not, I think, a trivial

1

one—that if you ask a historical question you will need historical evidence to answer it. Take, for example, a question of influence. According to Erwin Panofsky, Dürer's drawing, *The Death of Orpheus,*

derives from a Mantegnesque prototype transmitted through a North Italian engraving and probably inspired by a poetic source such as Politian's Orfeo.[1]

This conclusion must have been established (if it really *was* established) by a study of other objects besides the drawing itself and by inferences about presumable causal connections. Perhaps it is not necessary to defend here my terminological decision to separate art history from art criticism; the usage is convenient and does not commit anyone to substantive implications. My concern at the moment is to make an initial concession that if we want to know whether a North Italian engraving was in some way *causally* relevant to the existence and character of Dürer's drawing, then certain facts of history will be *logically* relevant, as supporting reasons, to a hypothesis we propose to prove.

There is another important kind of historical question that obviously calls for a historical—in this case, also, specifically an art-historical—inquiry. Part of our understanding, in a broad sense, of the artwork is seeing it in its significance for an artistic development: what it tells us about a particular stage in the painter's career (it may mark the emergence of a new style or subject matter), in the fulfillment or decline of an artistic period, in the history of the art of painting itself. It is light on such relationships that we perhaps principally hope for from art historians.

Setting explicitly and plainly historical questions aside, then, we turn to criticism proper. More interesting, and more debatable, is the claim that certain ahistorical questions can only be answered by appeal to historical evidence—or, more radically, that questions we have taken to be ahistorical are really historical questions in disguise. But at this point we need further distinctions. For there are several kinds of statement that occur characteristically in the discourse of critics, and what is relevant to one kind may not be relevant to another. The only safe course here, pedestrian as it may be, is to take these kinds one

2

by one, or in closely related groups. My examples will be chosen from pictorial art, but I am assuming that many of the problems they raise have analogues in other forms of art.

I

First, there are questions of meaning—semantic questions, in a broad sense. These may appear to be quite distinct from historical questions, since they are not questions about influence or significance, yet when we analyze them we may discover that they call for information about semantic conventions or rules of interpretation that were in force during some past period—conventions whose authority and jurisdiction can be established only by historical inquiry. For example, if we look into the meaning of the ostrich egg that hangs from the ceiling in a famous altarpiece by Piero della Francesca, we will find (according to the late art historian Millard Meiss) that ostriches were believed to be forgetful of their eggs, though later minded of them, and that consequently in the Middle Ages ostrich eggs were hung in churches to show how man, forgetful of his God, may, when illuminated by the Divine Light, return to God and be cherished.[2] (This is a good deal of meaning to attach to an egg—but, after all, ostrich eggs are large.) To interpret the egg in the painting is to say what such eggs meant in a particular religious community at the time the work was painted. It is historical scholarship that provides us with the rule of interpretation.

The symbolic ostrich egg exemplifies one familiar and important kind of artistic meaning. But we must not rush to generalize the conclusion to other kinds of meaning or reference. For example, before we can interpret the ostrich egg we must recognize that it *is* an ostrich egg; to establish this fact, however ("The painting represents an ostrich egg"), we appeal to knowledge, not of history, but of oölogy. To be sure, we must know something of ostrich eggs, but only in a timeless way: that there are such things and that they have a certain size and shape.

Do we not have to know at least this much of history: that a fifteenth-century Italian painter could have had access to ostrich eggs, or could have at least read about them, even if he never saw one? Here we encounter one of those unresolved issues that aesthetic questions are bound to lead to if they are faithfully

3

pursued. One way to put the problem is to ask whether something can be represented unintentionally. Suppose it could be proved, by historical inquiry, that Piero never saw and never heard about ostrich eggs: would we then have to conclude that the figure in his painting cannot represent an ostrich egg? I don't think we would. No doubt it is a little odd to think of someone's representing an object inadvertently, and this is perhaps very unlikely to happen; but I see no contradiction in the supposition. Dr. Seuss could conceivably invent an animal that later turns out to exist after all, though it is highly improbable that any of his creatures are really, as they say, viable. And Piero della Francesca could paint a shape that is a picture of an ostrich egg, though neither he nor his contemporaries could have recognized it as one—in which case, of course, it would not have the symbolic significance that Millard Meiss found, or at least suggested.

I want to defend a general claim here, in terms of a distinction that I have urged between portraying and depicting.[3] Briefly, what a painting portrays is this or that individual object or event: the Virgin Mary, the Annunciation. What it depicts is an object or event of a certain kind: a woman, an announcement by an angel. In general, to know what a painting portrays we must connect the painting with its object—we must know that the painter intended his work to refer to Mary and to a momentous event in her life, in which he believed and in which he expected his audience (or vidience?) to believe. So—in general—our understanding of what is portrayed rests essentially on historical knowledge of what once happened at some time prior to the painting of the work, or on historical knowledge of what was believed at the time of painting. But—again in general—our understanding of what is depicted is independent of historical knowledge. History is irrelevant to the question whether a painting depicts a woman or an ostrich egg.

But, you may say, what about angels? To recognize a depiction of an angel, we must know that angels have wings; and this knowledge does not come from personal observation. It is only by placing the artwork in a particular religious iconographic tradition that we can see it as depicting an angel rather than just as depicting some strangely winged man. Now, insofar as we appeal to existing texts about angels, we are not consulting history, but angelology, a branch of theology. But it seems that

4

we require more than this: we need to know what rules or conventions for depicting angels were accepted and employed in the time of the painting in question. And so it appears that angels, at least, may be an exception to my general claim about the ahistorical character of depiction.

Even if you are inclined to grant my general claim about the depiction of natural (or supernatural) things, you may argue that it breaks down when we turn to human artifacts. Imagine, for example, a painting that represents a trolley car (it might be a mural painting in the transportation building of some world's fair). Now, if you live in a city in which this mode of transit is not yet extinct, you clearly need no historical information to understand what the painting depicts. There are, of course, deep current issues about the precise nature of pictorial representation and whether or not it essentially involves a selective similarity between the picture and its object.[4] But in any case, your familiarity with the way trolley cars look enables you to read the picture. Even if in your city the ruthless hand of progress has cleared the streets of trolley cars, one of them may be preserved as a curiosity in a municipal museum. And though you may learn some history by going to the museum, you don't require that history to see that the object in the museum is of the sort depicted in the painting.

But suppose the trolleys are all gone, and all you know of them comes from a history of your city, with descriptions, perhaps illustrated by photographs, of what trolleys once were like. Then, in a sense, you are using historical knowledge to determine what the painting depicts—but only, I think, in too weak and insubstantial a sense to count against my claim that, in general, understanding of depiction does not depend on historical knowledge. For the only information that is relevant here is that such things as trolley cars have existed and have had certain characteristic features (wheels, windows, trolleys, front-rear symmetry, etc.). Knowledge of this sort is not strictly historical knowledge, since it is essentially dateless: you don't need to find out *when* the trolley cars came and went, or how, or why, any more than you need to find out when ostriches first appeared to recognize an ostrich egg depiction.

All this fussiness about exactly which statements about paintings are, and which are not, supported by historical information may seem unnecessary. But once we raise the question of the

5

relevance of history to criticism, we have, I believe, no alternative to patiently considering what critics would want to say and how they know these things to be true. We have not made any discoveries of great significance or novelty. Yet I think our distinctions can contribute toward fostering a greater judiciousness than sometimes characterizes discussions of our central question. It is easy to point out examples of historical relevance and then to wave the hand and conclude that practically every question for the critic is historical, or in the end reduces to history. My aim is to counteract this tendency, to try to carve out limited domains of independence for the critic—to see what is, in this respect, autonomous in art.

II

To point out what a painting depicts or portrays, and to interpret its symbolic significance, is surely (when such remarks are called for) within the province of the critic. Beyond that, we expect (both in the sense of predicting and in the sense of desiring) judgments of artistic goodness or aesthetic value. For example, in his book *On Quality in Art,* Jakob Rosenberg tells us that a drawing of an Oriental head by Martin Schongauer is a better drawing than another on a similar subject by one of his pupils. And he tells us why. Among other things,

> *There is no doubt that the Schongauer head has more plastic life, more surface animation and organic coherence than the other drawing. The whole and the parts are better related. . . . Altogether [in the pupil's work] we miss the graphic charm, the decorative coherence of the design, and the human animation that Schongauer achieves.*[5]

There might be some question about the correctness of Rosenberg's descriptions of the two drawings, and it must be conceded that the descriptions are quite general and somewhat vague. Nevertheless, Rosenberg is giving reasons for his conclusion, and relevant ones—and the conclusion of his argument appears to be independent of any historical evidence.

But perhaps this appearance is misleading. On one view of critical value judgments—a view that is, I believe, more common among historians of visual art than among historians of music or literature—a work of art is (or is to be regarded as) the solution of a "problem." Such problems are conceived in different ways, but the following may serve as examples: to create a satisfactory composition of two adults and a child, to capture the impression of bright sunlight on calm water, to break up a human body into an assemblage of cubist forms that suggest fundamental relationships of mass and at the same time make a coherent pattern. James Ackerman cites the illusionistic imitation of nature as a recurring artistic problem, and even proposes in such terms his account of style.

A style, then, may be thought of as a class of related solutions to a problem—or responses to a challenge—that may be said to begin whenever artists begin to pursue a problem or react to a challenge which differs significantly from those posed by the prevailing style or styles.[6]

If the problem is one posed by the art-historical situation at the time the work was created, then the artistic goodness or badness of that work is (or depends upon) its success in solving that problem. It follows that one cannot judge an art work until one has established, by historical inquiry, the nature of the problem it was designed to solve. We would have to know that the two drawings discussed by Rosenberg were both attempts to solve the same problem before we could determine which was the more successful, and why.

For various reasons, I do not accept this view of critical judgments, nor do I believe that even art historians could consistently adhere to it. In the first place, we often know nothing definite about the problems that may have existed and, existing, presented themselves to the artist and were acknowledged and addressed by him or her. Yet in such cases we often believe ourselves able to make judgments. Of course, given any painting, we may conceive and formulate some problem to which it can be regarded as a solution, just as, given any proposition, we may conceive of a question to which it could be an answer. But then we are really trying to decide what the work does that is worth doing, and the reference to a "problem" is otiose.

In the second place, we would often be able to think of various problems to which the painting could be a proposed solution; so we would get a multiplicity of perhaps conflicting judgments, among which we could not choose. Which suggests—to me, at least—that this is not the way to go about setting up the evaluative task.

In the third place, even when we *can* fix the historical context and the painter's intentions so that we can say quite exactly and

7

confidently what problem he was trying to solve, success or failure in this enterprise cannot determine artistic goodness. Depending on the fruitfulness and depth of the problem, a successful solution may be a magnificent or a trivial work of art.

Hence talk about historically set "artistic problems" readily passes out of the historical plane. Panofsky, for example, who speaks of such "problems," proceeds along these lines:

When we call a figure in an Italian Renaissance picture "plastic," while describing a figure in a Chinese painting as "having volume but no mass" (owing to the absence of "modeling"), we interpret these figures as two different solutions of a problem which might be formulated as "volumetric units (bodies) vs. illimited expanse (space)." ... Upon reflection it will turn out that there is a limited number of such primary problems, interrelated with each other, which on the one hand beget an infinity of secondary and tertiary ones, and on the other hand can be ultimately derived from one basic antithesis: differentiation vs. continuity.[7]

But it is clear that now we are no longer appealing to external historical information: the "problem" is derived from the painting itself, by applying a theoretical system articulating all possible "artistic problems." Of course it is true that we must have knowledge of many artworks to judge a particular artwork—we need a repertoire as background. But if the artworks in the repertoire (those from which Panofsky's system is derived) need not be of any particular time and place, we are not making use of them in their *historical* aspect. We have removed the concept of an "artistic problem" from something in the actual life-world of the painter, open to historical inquiry, to an ahistorical dimension or parameter of the art of painting.

I do not deny that we can frame various restricted or guarded sorts of value judgments that essentially involve historical comparisons; I only hold out for the existence of other value judgments ("This drawing is better than that") that are, so to speak, history-free, yet intelligible and arguable.

III

There is another way in which judgments of artistic value may be thought to rest on historical facts. Among the reasons that can be given in support of critical praise or denigration, as we see in the passage from Rosenberg, are descriptions of the

8

artwork in terms of its expressiveness, or what are now widely called "aesthetic qualities." "Plastic life," "organic coherence," and "graphic charm" are noted by Rosenberg as desirable qualities, found to a higher degree, or more intensely, in one drawing than in the other. But suppose it could be shown that we must undertake historical inquiry to discover whether in fact an artwork has such qualities, or whether it has them to a marked degree; then, indirectly, our evaluations would rest on historical evidence after all, for we could not know that Schongauer was a better draftsman than his pupil unless we could be confident that our perception of these qualities is not an illusion, but historically correct.

It is E. H. Gombrich who has opened up this extremely important and challenging line of argument. Though my formulation may reach a little beyond what he has explicitly stated, I hope it is free from distortion; in any case, it is well worth careful consideration on its merits. The conclusion is validly derived from three premises that are to be found in the final searching chapter of *Art and Illusion.*[8]

First, expressiveness involves matching; more explicitly, to say what a painting expresses we must select a description (or, more generally, a label) for its aesthetic quality. Thus, in Gombrich's celebrated example, a well-known painting by Mondrian is titled *Broadway Boogie-Woogie,* which assimilates it to Fats Waller playing *Doin' the Uptown Lowdown,* rather than, say, to Pablo Casals conducting Bach's *First Brandenburg Concerto.* We match the description with the painting.

Second, matching involves a selection among alternatives within sets of comparanda, that is, potential matchees and potential matchers. Thus, Gombrich says, we will accept the label *Boogie-Woogie* for this painting if we have to choose between this painting and a characteristic example of Mondrian's extremely still and rigid style; but we will accept the label *First Brandenburg Concerto* for this painting if we have to choose between this painting and an example of the Futurist Severini's feverish dynamism, and then we will willingly move the old label *Boogie-Woogie* over to the Severini. It is in contrast to Severini's that this painting is *First Brandenburg Concerto*-like.

From the first two premises Gombrich concludes that "we cannot judge expression without an awareness of the choice situation, without a knowledge of the organon."[9] Mondrian could make his multiplicity of red and yellow squares *Boogie-Woogie*-ish only because he was confining himself to a rectangular style in which most of the paintings consisted of fewer and larger elements.

Third, to know the comparanda that the painter actually had at hand—his range of objects to be matched and his repertoire of items to match with them—is to possess historical knowledge. Therefore, without appropriate historical knowledge we cannot determine what is expressed. Gombrich does not deny that we can often perceive aesthetic qualities in works of whose historical and cultural position we know nothing—say, Central African masks. But this is a mere impression, which needs to be confirmed, sometimes corrected, by historical inquiry, which sets bounds to what *could* be expressed at that time and place.[10] So a future visitor to the Museum of Modern Art might well notice a certain liveliness in the Mondrian painting, but he could not confidently call it "jazzy" unless he knew not only how this painting compared with other Mondrians but also how jazz (at the time Mondrian's artwork was painted) compared with other music.

This is a powerful and illuminating argument. Its only vulnerable, or at least questionable, point is the first premise. If that holds up, the conclusion seems secure.

Does expressiveness involve matching? If expressiveness consists in the exemplification of metaphorical labels, as in the theory of Nelson Goodman,[11] the answer is clearly yes. But if we distinguish between properties and the predicates that are used to describe them, we must say that the *properties* need not involve matching merely because the application of *predicates* involves a matching of words to things. This issue need not detain us, however, for the distinction, even if sound, will not help much. We got into the problem of expressiveness, you will recall, by considering the reasons that Rosenberg gave for his comparative value judgment: the thesis we started out to investigate is that artistic value judgments indirectly rest on historical evidence because some of their reasons (that is, those ascribing aesthetic qualities) do. When we give a reason—when we say that the Schongauer drawing has "surface animation" (like *Broadway Boogie-Woogie*)—we are clearly matching a description with an object, and if this matching requires historical knowledge, Gombrich's conclusion must be accepted.

10

The equation has two ends; let us begin by looking at the predicates that are to be selected from. No doubt our descriptions of aesthetic qualities are implicitly comparative; Rosenberg's decision to build his book on pairs of readily comparable artworks takes advantage of this fact. We speak of paintings as more or less animated, as hardly at all animated or as highly animated; and no doubt in such judgments we have in the back of our minds a rough norm or standard, either medium or extreme cases. Moreover, "animated" belongs to a family of predicates, the rest of which we more or less consciously rejected: "static," "sluggish," "turbulent," etc. Now it might be argued that our choice from among these predicates must be at least partly governed by historical considerations, since we must limit ourselves to predicates (or to synonyms of predicates) that were available at the time the painting was painted: or, that we have no right (it would be anachronistic) to call the painting "animated" unless we know that the painter could have intended his audience to describe it by this or some equivalent term.

The rationale for such a view would presumably be based on some notion of "communication"—a slippery term in contexts such as this. One would say that the painter intended to convey the concept of animation, and had to know that those who would see his painting could read this concept from it: so if asked what the painting expressed, they could say it was "decidedly animated," or something of the sort. But I think this model of painting and of painting appreciation has serious difficulties and that it unduly limits the art itself. A painting may have subtle and valuable aesthetic qualities that we have no very apt labels for; the purpose of painting cannot be to get people to utter descriptions. And a painting may have qualities that viewers many years later can describe more fully and more precisely than could the painter or his contemporaries (for example, because jazz and the word "jazzy" have come into existence). So I see no solid justification for imposing on our descriptions of paintings such historical limits.

I turn now to the works themselves: what must we know about their historical context in order to choose correctly from among the descriptive predicates now available? One line of argument on this point is that we must know what alternative ways of painting were open to the painter, considering the art-historical situation, the style in which he chose to work, the

11

range of qualities possible to his medium, etc. Thus, if we learned that the Schongauer drawing was the *most* animated one that could be made by him, we should apply our most extreme predicate and describe it, say, as "turbulent." This argument cannot be right, for its conclusion is absurd. Anyone who holds that to describe an artwork correctly we must contrast it with others painted at its time or just before—call this a "contrastive class"—must tell us how to form the proper class. Shall we select only works of the same artist? But then we would not be in a position to describe his style generally, in contrast to other styles—to speak, for example, of a painting as one of Perugino's "utterly serene compositions."[12] If we admit all contemporaneous paintings to the contrastive class we shall not then be able to say that, in general, the period featured certain aesthetic qualities to a high degree. The only unquestionable contrastive class is the class of *all* other paintings; but in this class no painting has a privileged place on account of its historical position.

The problem of specifying the contrastive class[13] is brought out by one of Gombrich's very interesting examples, which we are perhaps not meant to take very seriously. He discusses a painting by Kandinsky, called *At Rest* (1928, Guggenheim Museum), in which, according to one authority, Kandinsky "wanted the shapes themselves to suggest and convey the feeling of calm or repose." These are Gombrich's words,[14] and I regard them as a little misleading: it is not that Kandinsky wanted his painting to make the viewer *feel* calm, but that he wanted his painting to *look* calm, to have the quality of repose. This is no verbal quibble, for Gombrich claims that Kandinsky did not succeed: "I certainly doubt that even the most sensitive beholder would feel 'at rest' in front of this picture." I doubt that, too, but it doesn't mark the painting as a failure, for it is equally true of any painting you can name. I am sure Gombrich would agree that paintings are not sedatives or tranquilizers. The real question, then, is whether, by arranging the rectangles and triangles that make up his vaguely-suggested harbor scene, Kandinsky succeeded in giving his picture the emergent aesthetic quality of calm or repose.

Though Gombrich apparently does not think we can see restfulness in this painting when we consider it by itself, he does think we can come to see it if we approach the painting with the relevant historical (here, biographical) knowledge.

12

It so happens, however, that we can restore a clear expressive meaning to Kandinsky's composition by placing it in its historical context. During the 'twenties', the artist worked side by side with Paul Klee at the Bauhaus, and the two were friends. . . . Now, in 1927, Klee . . . had experimented with the suggestion of movement in ships, first in a drawing of slightly swaying sailing boats and then in a larger harbour scene which he called "Activity of the Port" . . . [1927, Berne, Klee Foundation]. It is a witty experiment in conveying the bustle and restlessness of the harbour by novel graphic means. What is relevant to our context is only how much Kandinsky's work, painted a year later, gains in intelligibility when placed side by side with Klee's. Suddenly the massive rectangular forms acquire indeed the dimensions of heaviness and calm.[15]

This is an interesting experiment, but what does it prove? It proves that if you approach Kandinsky's painting after just having looked at one with a great deal of busy movement in it, it will look very calm—more than if you had just been looking at a gallery full of Ruysdael landscapes. But, first, I doubt that this would happen if the Kandinsky did not already have a good deal of stability and fixedness in its forms and composition. And second, I don't see that the historical context is at all essential; the same effect can be achieved by first looking at any painting that is full of activity; the historical facts that Klee was a friend and that his painting was done in 1927 don't seem to matter. And third, I note that Klee's painting is described as restless and bustling (or at least these are qualities conveyed); but apparently the perception of *these* aesthetic qualities does not depend on a historical contrast with any earlier picture.

My treatment of Gombrich's account of expression must omit many of the provocative and penetrating points he has made in various essays—and it must also resist the temptation to open up further discussion on other points that I would like to see more fully explained. I have been convinced by Gombrich that artistic expressiveness is sometimes closely related to—and even bound up with—communication, in what is now its technical Colin Cherry sense. One of Gombrich's best examples of contrast in communication is from *Ali Baba*: when the thief marked one door with chalk, the sign-value of that mark, since it depended entirely on contrast with the unmarked doors, was easily destroyed by marking all the other doors in the same way.[16] The signification of the X depended on contrast; but signification is

13

not, of course, the same thing as expressiveness. The *Ali Baba* example does not involve expressiveness at all. A Quaker meetinghouse signifies its builders' commitment to a way of life just by virtue of its contrast with the more elaborate churches and chapels of other sects; but the expressiveness of any particular Quaker meetinghouse is not cancelled by the building of others no less plain, sturdy, simple, and spare.

Thus I can't help thinking that Gombrich goes too far in his understandable effort to counteract art historians who have not understood the essential role of choice in artistic signification. Discussing a book by Charles Stirling, he quotes some of the author's descriptions of seventeenth-century Dutch paintings, and comments:

All these descriptions depend on the author's knowledge of alternatives. What was "bourgeois opulence" in seventeenth-century Holland would have been beyond the dreams of a twelfth-century nobleman. But the "intimacy" of these motifs still stands out when compared to the typical repertoire of contemporary Flemish artists, the peacocks, game and silver dishes of Snyders. Naturally these in their turn would not be particularly "heroic" (no courage was needed to paint them) if they were not so much larger and louder than the average Dutch counterpart, in other words if their deviation from some expected median were not felt to be equivalent to the similar deviations of other "heroic" genres in literature or music. Likewise, if there is indeed "serenity" in Caravaggio and humility in Spanish still lifes this character must also spring from their place within the field of possibilities. For neither the words nor the labels used by the critics have any of these meanings inherently and by themselves. They only communicate meaning within an articulated tradition.[18]

The problem of the contrastive class is that of specifying the relevant "field of possibilities," short of considering the entire range of existing paintings as constituting that field. I do not see what the criterion could be. Meanwhile, it is certainly true that an animal that is large when compared to a mouse may be small when compared to an elephant, but we can still roughly convey the size of an animal by saying that it is about as large as a breadbox. And the statement that one painting is more serene than another may hold up, whatever other paintings may come into our ken.

I do not, of course, consider myself to have disproved Gombrich's account of expression. My concern has been to articulate some of the difficulties I find in it, in the hope of contributing to their resolution, by that account or another.

IV

Though it will add nothing substantive to my argument, I hope I may be indulged in one more example, which I offer as a final warning against overemphasis on the relevance of historical knowledge to art criticism. As a foil to my little sermon, I begin with a quotation from that admirable critic, Frank Getlein, writing in *The New Republic* about the Archives of American Art, which the Detroit Institute of Arts set up as a repository of historical facts about the works of American painters, including tape recordings of interviews with painters and their companions. Getlein remarked that some might regard all this as beside the point, but "Everything we know about an artist or his times contributes something to our understanding of his work."[19] It is always easy, and therefore unrewarding, to overturn such sweeping universal generalizations, but in this case I want not only to state explicitly that Getlein's statement is false but also to add that it would be more nearly true if he had added "or *mis*understanding" to "understanding."

Some years ago there was an interesting symposium, later published, at a meeting of the American Society for Aesthetics, in which Picasso's *Night Fishing at Antibes* (Museum of Modern Art) was discussed by a psychologist, a philosopher, and an art historian.[20] What the art historian, George Levitine, said is, to my mind, a direct counterexample to Getlein's generalization, though I don't think it did any real harm, except in so far as it distracted attention from the work at hand. In search of understanding, he cast about for a "filiation," or possible source, to compare with the Picasso. He was reminded of paintings by Raphael and Copley, but without enthusiasm; finally he came up with *The Bathers*, a seventeenth-century Dutch painting in the Louvre, somewhat hesitantly attributed to Nicolas Maes. It shows a gang of country boys swimming off an old boat. Unfortunately, there is no fishing in it, but there are features that are vaguely similar to those in *Night Fishing at Antibes*. Levitine concluded that Picasso had been influenced by this painting, and suggested that the recognition of this influence "can perhaps cast a light upon the mechanics of some of Picasso's distortions."[21]

15

There is no doubt that there are distortions—the flounder that is being speared is no Mediterranean species, but only a Picasso species, and the girls watching from the jetty are most unusual, despite the normality of the double ice cream cone: one has seven fingers on one hand, the other has an eye that seems to have dropped to her chin. But what are these distortions distortions *from?* In paintings that are explicitly allusive—as in Picasso's series of variations on *Las Meninas* or on *The Woman of Algiers*—an acquaintance with the original painting is called for, so we may see what changes Picasso made for his own purposes. But the expressiveness of the distortions in *Night Fishing at Antibes*, as far as I can see, does not depend on their deviation from earlier pictures or styles of depiction, but from flounders and females as we are acquainted with them in the real world. Levitine said many interesting and helpful things about *Night Fishing at Antibes*, but I believe none of them owes anything to the art history he invokes.

In his discussion, Rudolph Arnheim made many perceptive comments on the shapes and figures in the painting, but when he came to the "paradoxical contradiction between the nature of the action represented and the dynamics of the shapes representing,"[22] he was suddenly moved to reflection of a very different sort.

It seems legitimate to remember here that the painting was done in August 1939, when the imminence of World War II darkened the horizon. In this ominous light, the murder of the fishes, portrayed in our painting, acquires a particular meaning. Watched with non-committal curiosity by the girls, whom we described as creatures of pleasure and luxury, the prospect of slaughter appears unreal, paralyzed in its impact by its remoteness, by the incompatibility of violence with the gay setting of the Mediterranean harbor. . . . The foreboding of violent, but unknown, things to come emerges as the dominant theme of the painting.[23]

Here are two historical facts: (1) the painting was painted in August, 1939, and (2) the Germans invaded Poland on September 1. This is the knowledge, I would say, that serves only to darken our understanding of this painting.

If we were not told beforehand that we must look at this painting in an "ominous light" and find it full of "foreboding" and "violence," I think we would find it most delightfully cheerful. True, the man on the right (unlike his apparently sea-

16

sick and retching companion) is certainly concentrating with fierce—even with absurd—intensity on spearing the flounder. But can we describe this imminent capture as "murder" and "slaughter"? This flatfish is the most unlikely symbol of suffering humanity that one could conjure up. It reminds me of what Harold Ross once said about the classic *New Yorker* cartoon in which the severed head of a duellist says "Touché." The cartoon was originally drawn by Carl Rose, but Ross thought it was too gruesome. Let Thurber draw it, he said; "Thurber's people don't bleed." We may be sure that Picasso's fish doesn't bleed, either. As for the girls—one of whom does indeed give promise of pneumatic bliss, like T. S. Eliot's Grushenka—they are hardly to be cast in the role of those who dance into the dawn of disaster, like Byron's midnight revellers before Waterloo, or Shaw's doomed denizens of Heartbreak House, or the travelling players in *Idiot's Delight*.

Of course knowledge is, from the most fundamental perspective, always better than ignorance. We cannot have too much. But knowledge misdirected can lead to its polar opposite, which is not ignorance, but false belief. And misdirection is always a matter of taking as logically relevant what is, in fact, not so.

Notes

1. Erwin Panofsky, "Albrecht Dürer and Classical Antiquity," in *Meaning in the Visual Arts: Papers in and on Art History* (Garden City, N.Y.: Doubleday and Company, 1955), p. 239. For many other examples, see Göran Hermerén, *Influence in Art and Literature* (Princeton, N.J.: Princeton University Press, 1975).

2. See Millard Meiss, *"Ovum Struthionis:* Symbol and Allusion in Piero della Francesca's Montefeltro Altarpiece," in *The Painter's Choice: Problems in Interpretation of Renaissance Art* (New York: Harper and Row, 1976), p. 107.

3. Monroe C. Beardsley, *Aesthetics: Problems in the Philosophy of Criticism* (New York: Harcourt Brace Jovanovich, 1958), chap. 6.

4. See Nelson Goodman, *Languages of Art* (Indianapolis: Bobbs-Merrill, 1968), chapter 1. Compare with Monroe C. Beardsley, "Languages of Art and Art Criticism," *Erkenntnis* 12(1978):95–118.

5. Jakob Rosenberg, *On Quality in Art: Criteria of Excellence, Past and Present* (Princeton, N.J.: Princeton University Press, 1967), p. 133.

6. James S. Ackerman, "A Theory of Style," in Monroe C. Beardsley and Herbert M. Schueller, eds., *Aesthetic Inquiry* (Belmont, Calif.: Dickinson, 1967), p. 64.

7. Erwin Panofsky, "The History of Art as a Humanistic Discipline," in *Meaning in the Visual Arts*, p. 21.

8. E. H. Gombrich, "From Representation to Expression," *Art and Illusion*, 2nd ed. (Princeton, N.J.: Princeton University Press, 1961); see also several of the essays in his *Meditations on a Hobby Horse*, 2nd ed. (London: Phaedon, 1971).

9. *Art and Illusion*, p.376.

10. Ibid., p. 388. See also *Meditations*, pp. 96–97.

11. Goodman, *Languages of Art*, chap. 2.

12. *Meditations*, p. 91.

13. This problem is also discussed by Richard Wollheim, *Art and Its Objects* (New York: Harper and Row, 1968), pp. 48–57.

14. *Meditations*, p. 67.

15. Ibid., p. 68.

16. Ibid., p. 111.

17. Compare with *Meditations*, p. 17.

18. *Meditations*, p. 100.

19. June 27, 1960.

20. Rudolf Arnheim, Douglas N. Morgan, and George Levitine, "Picasso's *Night Fishing at Antibes*," *Journal of Aesthetics and Art Criticism* 22 (Winter 1963): 165–75.

21. Ibid., p. 174.

22. Ibid., p. 166.

23. Ibid., p. 167.

Philosophy
and
History

Karsten Harries

I

Most recent philosophy has been ahistorical in orientation. Even when dealing with inherited problems the tendency has been to lift such problems out of their context, to draw a sharp distinction between history—more particularly the history of philosophy—and philosophy. But can philosophy afford to divorce itself from history? I would like to approach this question with an example.

In the preface to the *Tractatus*, Wittgenstein explains his failure to give the reader an adequate accounting of his sources by declaring that whether what he has thought was thought before him by another is a matter of indifference to him. Given our nervous obsession with originality we may find it difficult not to suspect behind this profession of indifference an "anxiety of influence," behind the paucity of references to the work of others a desperate assertion of self in the face of the overwhelming weight of the past.

A closer look at Wittgenstein's biography makes it a bit difficult to see how he could have been overly burdened by his knowledge of the philosophical tradition. Wittgenstein knew little of the history of philosophy. This is not necessarily a criticism; the originality and freshness of the *Tractatus* are due, in part at least, to Wittgenstein's ignorance of the traditional answers to many of the problems with which he was concerned. In spite of an early acquaintance with Schopenhauer's *The World as Will and Representation* and in spite of careful study of the work of Russell and Frege, Wittgenstein was able to philosophize almost *de novo*. At times the *Tractatus* reminds one of the Presocratics or of Descartes. One has the same sense of witnessing a beginning. A certain naiveté or, if not that, at least an ability to forget and put aside our books, may be necessary today if we are to escape from what Nietzsche calls the fate of having been born with grey hairs.

By now the *Tractatus,* too, has been placed in its historical context. If the facts of his indebtedness were a matter of professed indifference to Wittgenstein, many of his readers did not share that indifference and provided the missing footnotes. Perhaps it was curiosity, innocent delight in discovering precursors and influences, that gave birth to such scholarship. Some readers may have felt a need to legitimate the work and their interest in it by providing it with a noble ancestry, while others, having been born with grey hairs, may have wanted to defend themselves against genuine creativity by putting it in its (historical) place.

But what should all of this matter to the philosopher? How important is it, when reading a philosophical text, to know its background and sources? How important is it, for example, to know what Wittgenstein learned from Kant and from Schopenhauer, from Hertz and from Frege? If one is interested in Wittgenstein's originality, such questions, of course, are relevant. But do they have a bearing on the truth of what is being said? And should this not be the proper concern of the philosopher? What is the philosophical significance of such historical scholarship?

There is a ready answer: such scholarship helps us to understand better what is being said in the text. Every philosopher has to express himself in a language that is rooted in a particular tradition. Without knowledge of that tradition we find ourselves in the position of someone who wants to read a poem without quite having mastered the language in which it is written. Such mastery is not easily separated from insight into a particular way of life. Especially when reading a text belonging to an unfamiliar past, a certain amount of historical knowledge is an indispensable condition of understanding. The same would seem to be true of philosophical texts. Learning a philosopher's sources can be likened to learning a language. Knowledge of these sources helps to make us more discerning readers.

But while this must be granted, the pursuit of sources is easily carried too far. The interest in precursors and influences may drown the philosophical thought in its historical context. Instead of helping us to a better understanding of *what* is being said, it may focus our attention only on *how* it is said, and thus obscure what is essential with accidental detail. Thus when Wittgenstein likens the *Tractatus* to a ladder that one must throw away once one has climbed it, he may well be expressing his thoughts by means of an image borrowed from Mauthner. But does it really matter? Is what he is saying not clear enough?

Just as some would claim that one need not know the historical place of a work of art to be able to judge its aesthetic value, can one also maintain, and with greater justification, that we need not know the sources of a thinker to understand what he thought? In the case of art one can argue that judgments of beauty depend on an apprehension of form involving faculties that belong to all human beings and that are not tied to a particular time or place. This is essentially Kant's position. His extreme formalism implies that a pure aesthetic judgment may not take into account the historical situation of artist or observer. And should judgments of truth not be similarly pure? Thus when a proposition is said to be true, it is not said to be true relative only to a certain time and place. The Pythagorean theorem is not true today and false tomorrow, nor does it matter whether it is expressed in Greek or in English.

Perhaps we should insist, as Wittgenstein does in the *Tractatus,* that a distinction be drawn between what is being thought and the way in which what is being thought is expressed. Wittgenstein's ladder image would seem to belong to the latter. It is therefore dispensable; another perhaps even more telling expression could take its place. In the preface to the *Tractatus* Wittgenstein is thus quite ready to grant that he may not have succeeded in expressing his thoughts as clearly as possible. "Here I

21

am conscious that I have fallen far short of the possible. Simply because my powers are insufficient to cope with the task.—May others come and do it better." One is reminded of Kant's willingness to admit in his prefaces to both the first and the second edition of *The Critique of Pure Reason* that his manner of representation left room for considerable improvement. But both Kant and the young Wittgenstein insisted that inadequacy of expression does not affect the sense, and thus the truth, of what is being expressed; such inadequacy affects only its communicability. The pursuit of truth would indeed seem to demand a certain indifference to expression. In this respect science differs from poetry. Wittgenstein remarks in the *Philosophical Investigations:*

531. We speak of understanding a sentence in the sense in which it can be replaced by another which says the same; but also in the sense in which it cannot be replaced by any other. (Any more than one musical theme can be replaced by another.)

In the one case the thought in the sentence is something common to different sentences; in the other, something that is expressed only by these words in these positions. (Understanding a poem.)

This suggests that discourse can be placed on a spectrum marked by two poles. At the poetic pole it is impossible to draw a distinction between expression and thought, while at the scientific pole such a distinction is demanded.[1] To grasp the sense of a scientific proposition is to know also that nothing essential is lost when that proposition is restated in different words or translated into another language. As Frege puts this point: "The thought, in itself immaterial, clothes itself in the material garment of a sentence and thereby becomes comprehensible to us."[2] Frege's "thoughts" are thus not part of the sensible world, nor are they dependent on particular acts of thinking. Such acts of thinking, which psychology or history might investigate, could grasp a "thought," but as the word *grasps* suggests, "thoughts" transcend concrete thinking. "Thoughts" may remain unthought, they can be discovered or be forgotten, they can be well- or ill-expressed, but their truth or falsity does not depend on these elements.

On this view "thoughts" are not subject to time; truth does not have a history. We can speak of history only on the level of expressions. To emphasize the history of a science would thus be to emphasize what is unessential. Do we need to know the history of geometry to understand geometry? And just as an obvious distinction can be drawn between the practitioner of a science and its historian, should we not also draw a sharp distinction between the philosopher and the historian of philosophy? Given an interest in a truth, the history of its discovery (and, with it, the question of originality) should have no real importance. It would thus appear that when Wittgenstein professes indifference about whether his thoughts had been thought before him by someone else, he is speaking as anyone should speak whose concern is truth. Philosophy appears to demand a certain indifference to history.

Unfortunately the matter is not quite that simple. It is significant that in this same preface Wittgenstein is not willing to claim that the truth of what he has asserted is unassailable and definitive. He is content to settle for the more modest claim that what he has asserted seems true to him. As a matter of fact, he was soon to question his own earlier assertions.

The history of the development of Wittgenstein's thinking invites us to raise the question: Is a transhistorical truth available to man? Is the conception of such a truth not perhaps just an idea which, while it may haunt man, will finally elude him? How are we to distinguish between the truth and what only *seems* to us to be the truth because of our particular situation? This question is closely tied to another: Can we finally distinguish pure thoughts from their expressions? Frege was keenly aware of this difficulty: "I cannot put a thought in the hands of my readers with the request that they should minutely examine it from all sides. I have to content myself with presenting the reader with a thought, in itself immaterial, dressed in sensible linguistic form. The metaphorical aspect of language presents difficulties. The sensible always breaks in and makes expression metaphorical and so improper."[3] But if expression is always improper, how are we to disentangle thoughts and expressions?

An example may help to clarify what is at issue. Descartes insists that, no matter what my situation, I cannot doubt that I, a thinking substance, exist and, he adds, what makes it impossible for me to do so is nothing other than the clarity and distinctness of the idea involved. Here, then, we would appear to grasp a simple truth, uncontaminated by anything tied to the particular situation of the thinker. But do we in fact have a clear and distinct idea of ourselves as a thinking substance? To be sure, we have to grant that our existence cannot be doubted, but how much content can we give to this knowledge? Descartes points to the supposedly clear and distinct idea I have of myself as a thinking substance. Do I recognize myself in that idea? At most it offers me the abstract form of my and any other consciousness, an abstraction which can appear so clear and distinct only because it is so formal and empty. As soon as I try to grasp myself as this individual, existing here and now, the illusion of transparency disappears.

As a matter of fact, even that abstraction is less than clear and distinct. Descartes's interpretation of the self as a thinking substance can be shown to rest on a quite traditional, but questionable, interpretation of being which says that "to be" means first of all to be as a substance. Like the young Wittgenstein, Descartes wanted to think for himself, free from the distortions of what others have said and taken for granted. He wanted to begin with the beginning. It was for this reason that he resolved to seek no other science than that which he could find in himself and in the great book of the world.[4]

From the very beginning that attempt proved impossible. No matter how hard Descartes tried, no matter how self-consciously he went about bracketing the authority of what others had thought and written before him, in the end he could not escape the tyranny of the past. On further reflection what is presented as a clear and distinct intuition often appears to be a verbal construction that derives much of its authority from other words. The more carefully we reflect on what Descartes has written, the more entangled intuition and reliance on the words of others become. Should we consider this a failing that a more careful philosopher could have avoided? Or is it simply the human condition that denies man vision unclouded by the past?

What then is the relevance of history to philosophy? So far I have done little more than point to a certain hostility between philosophical and historical reflection: while the philosopher has often aspired to a point of view that would allow him to survey reality *sub specie aeternitatis,* history has tended to mock such aspirations. Historical reflection helps to cure the philosopher's hubris. Can philosophy survive this cure? But what is philosophy?

24

II

In the first book of the *Metaphysics* Aristotle claims that "it is owing to their wonder that men both now begin and at first began to philosophize; they wondered originally at obvious difficulties, then advanced little by little and stated difficulties about the greater matters, e.g. about the phenomena of the moon and those of the sun and the stars, and about the genesis of the universe."[5] Philosophy is said to have its origin in those familiar dislocations that are inseparable from everyday experience: a tool is not in its place, the roof is leaking, we discover that some time ago we took the wrong turn. We all run into difficulties that force us to look up from what we have been doing in order to determine where we are, what possibilities are open to us, and what is to be done. There is, of course, a decisive difference between these "obvious difficulties" and "the greater matters" that concern the philosopher. While "obvious difficulties" receive their significance from the projects which are part of life, "greater matters," Aristotle tells us, are pursued only to escape from ignorance. The philosopher has taken leave from the world and its cares and concerns; he stands beside it as a mere observer.

This leave-taking renders philosophy problematic. It is no accident that the familiar image of the absent-minded philosopher is as old as philosophy itself. In Plato's *Theaetetus* we find the anecdote of the pretty Thracian servant-girl who mocked Thales for falling into a well while gazing at the mysteries of the sky. Socrates tells his story about the founder of philosophy to illustrate that only the "outer form" of the philosopher is in the city; "the mind, disdaining the littlenesses and nothingnesses of human things, is 'flying all abroad' as Pindar says, measuring earth and heaven and the things which are under and on the earth and above the heaven, interrogating the whole nature of each and all in their entirety, but not condescending to anything which is within reach."[6]

But does man have this power of flight? We may well wonder whether, searching for his higher truths, the philosopher does not become another Icarus. Aristotle himself asks whether the kind of knowledge claimed by philosophy should not be "regarded as beyond human power: for in many ways human nature is in bondage, so that according to Simonides 'God alone can have this privilege,' and it is unfitting that man should not be content to seek the knowledge that is suited to him."[7] The philosopher's search for knowledge makes him a rival of God. There is a suggestion of hubris, a suspicion that the knowledge claimed by the philosopher may not belong to man. But Aristotle dismisses such qualms. God is not jealous. Nor is such inquiry unnatural, for "all men by nature desire to know." They desire to know not because such knowledge might prove useful or help them find the right way; knowledge is not in need of such justifications. It is its own reward.

On this view the dignity of philosophy is inseparable from its uselessness. Because it is not good for anything else, because it "exists for its own sake," philosophy is "the only free science" and as such it is the worthy occupation of free men. Both Plato and Aristotle insist on this connection between freedom and philosophy. Not only does the pursuit of truth require free time—only a man of leisure can be a philosopher—but, more importantly, it is precisely because the philosopher does not approach things with a particular end in mind that he is able to see them with more open eyes. And only because he has freed himself from the rule of the body and the senses, because he is able to "fly all abroad" to distant places and times, indeed beyond all place and all time—can he rise to a knowledge of universals and gain an objective understanding of what is.

But the question returns: does man have such power of flight? It must be answered with a guarded "yes." Anticipation, memory, and imagination show that man does indeed transcend his situation. My location here and now is not a prison. Although I recognize that I see the world from a particular point of view, i.e., as perspectival appearance, such recognition presupposes that I am in some sense already beyond these perspectives. Thus as I look at that tree over there it is easy to imagine how it would look given different points of view. And if the imagination thus transcends the limits of the senses and the accident of the body's location, thought reaches even further. All the different appearances of the tree can be understood as appearances of the same object, an object which, while it presents itself to us in countless appearances, can only be thought. The transcendence of thought over sensation and imagination mirrors itself in the distinction between reality and appearance.

Similarly I can think of my historical situation as providing a point of view that lets me experience things in certain ways. The shape of the modern world provides us with something like a cultural *a priori*. Our spiritual situation is not that of the Middle Ages. As I learn about that other world I also gain a clearer understanding of the perspectival nature of my own. By presenting us with different points of view history prevents us from falsely absolutizing what happens to be our own. At the same time it invites a search for descriptions that have left historical relativity behind. Historical reflection appears here as no more than a preparation for the work of the philosopher.

Constitutive of man is the ability to transcend any perspective he recognizes as a perspective. This makes it possible to oppose to the concrete "I" and its vision of the world a transcendental or pure "I" whose "vision" of the world would be aperspectival and *sub specie aeternitatis*. The idea of such an "I" is implicit in our experience. It can be uncovered and made the measure of our descriptions of the things we encounter. What we take to be the case can be given its measure in what such an ideal observer would find true—where it is important to note that the ideal observer need not exist to function as such a measure. Using that measure the phenomena presented to us by our senses have to be judged to be no more than perspectival appearance. If we want to do justice to reality we have to employ forms of description from which all those aspects relative to a particular point of view—including all secondary qualities—have been eliminated. Only such descriptions are truly objective, i.e., scientific.

Heidegger has suggested that all this talk of a pure or transcendental "I" rests on an illegitimate secularization of the traditional concept of God.[8] And it is, of course, true that there are systematic and historical connections between the Christian God and the pure I. But to point this out is not to discredit the latter conception. The pure I has its foundation in the self-understanding of the concretely existing individual, who, as he becomes aware of himself as limited by a particular point of view, also discovers within himself the power to transcend this limitation. Man is haunted by the idea of a vision free from the accident of the body's location in space and time. The transcendental I beckons him with the promise of a place where he can stand without danger that this place, too, will prove to be relative. The success of our science makes it impossible to dismiss this promise as a mere dream.

Unlike God, man can think, but cannot occupy this place. He can demand objectivity of his descriptions of the world, but he possesses no organ to match that demand. Thus science depends for its content on perspectival experience, although, by imposing on this content its more objective form, it is able to claim to offer a more adequate representation of reality. Still, we have no pure vision. In the absence of such vision the pursuit of the pure I threatens man with a loss of place. For in that I man grasps himself not as he is, but as the form of all that he might possibly be. With such transcendental reflection the place which he actually occupies becomes only one of infinitely many possible places, his way of life one of infinitely many possible ways of life. If man's self-transcendence allows him to turn towards objectivity and to search for the truth beyond appearance, inseparable from this turn is an understanding of the world *sub specie possibilitatis,* i.e., as groundless. Reality is reduced to opaque facticity, human existence to a dislocated, free-floating freedom that cannot discover its proper place, the ethos which would permit it to come to rest. The pursuit of objectivity leads to nihilism. The price of the philosopher's flight to the heaven of pure thought is a loss of meaning.

III

This connection between transcendental reflection and nihilism invites reconsideration of Simonides' challenge that the knowledge sought by the philosopher is not suited to man. Heidegger pointedly juxtaposes Aristotle's claim that "all men by nature desire to know" with Augustine's critique of the appetite of knowledge, which lets "men go on to search out the hidden powers of nature [which is besides our end], and which profits not, and wherein men desire nothing but to know."[9] Theoretical inquiry divorced from practice is seen here as an inauthentic activity, which instead of leading man to a clearer understanding of his vocation is itself an indication that this vocation has been neglected.

Augustine's association of that desire for knowledge that Aristotle ties to human nature with sinful curiosity resurfaces in the later Wittgenstein's critique of philosophy. Philosophical problems, Wittgenstein remarks in the *Investigations,* have the form "I don't know my way about."[10] To be sure, not all problems having that form are therefore philosophical: just as Aristotle dis-

28

tinguishes everyday difficulties from the "greater matters" that occupy the philosopher, we have to distinguish the philosopher's loss of place from what we usually mean when we say that someone does not know his way about. But while according to Aristotle it is man's own nature that leads him to philosophy, Wittgenstein claims that the philosopher is someone who has been led astray by the appearance of language.

Language liberates us from what immediately presents itself. Beyond what is actually given it opens up an infinite space of possibilities. Language-use and a measure of self-transcendence and freedom are inseparable. That man can use language presupposes some distance between himself and his situation. Similarly it presupposes a contrast between the infinite complexity of life and the comparative simplicity of language. Yet while this contrast is essential to language—if the same linguistic signs could not be used in different, although in some respects similar situations, language would be superfluous—it may be a source of confusion and is easily exaggerated when language is divorced from the larger contexts of which it is usually a part. Thus the fact that the same word may be used to describe countless particulars may suggest that there must be some essence beyond time and place in which all these particulars participate. Language itself invites the philosopher's flight to the universal and eternal.

According to Wittgenstein, philosophy arises when man allows himself to become bewitched by language and, as a result, loses his place in the language-games of the everyday. As the unity "of language and the actions into which it is woven" that characterizes ordinary language is destroyed, language begins to "idle" or go "on a holiday."[11] The charge is familiar. From the very beginning the philosopher's disinterested curiosity that leads him to build his castles in the clouds, claiming timeless validity for his constructions, has been subjected to questioning and ridicule. The philosopher's reply is equally familiar: must we not be willing to forsake the uncertain ground furnished by what is usually taken for granted if we are to discover a firmer ground? But has philosophy ever found such firmer ground? Its history seems to lend support to Wittgenstein's contention that all such attempts must fail and that the forsaken ground can be regained only by returning to that mode of life and discourse from which the philosopher has departed.

In places Wittgenstein suggests that the philosopher's departure from ordinary language is rather like an unfortunate accident or a disease that has befallen him and from which he must be cured. But that cannot be quite right. Augustine is closer to the mark when he places theoretical inquiry in the context of sin and thus recognizes that its pursuit is not simply an accident that has overtaken us, but that its pursuit is something we will. If philosophy is indeed a misfortune, it is one that we ourselves have chosen. Philosophy begins with the refusal simply to accept things in all their confusing variety and mutability and with a search for some reality that can stem confusion and time and that can justify human existence.

Man demands of himself an account that places phenomena on firm ground. This demand leads to attempts to escape from those conditions that subject man to time and accident. In thought, at least, man seeks for his true home beyond the accident of historical and spatial location. We are now in a position to understand better what it is that lets Wittgenstein call philosophy an obsession. It is not simply that we are bewitched by language: our inability to accept the temporality of human existence lets us *want* to be bewitched.

In spite of philosophy's noble ancestry, which leads us back to Plato and beyond, how can the philosopher's hope that he will uncover the timeless essence of things be justified? Wittgenstein's critique of traditional philosophy rests on a conviction, never really defended, that no justification can be given. Nor do we need philosophy. Our language is quite in order as it is. This shifts the burden away from ordinary language and experience and places it instead on philosophy. It is the philosopher who has to justify his use of language. To justify is to point to that in which what is to be justified has its ground. The only ground that Wittgenstein admits is ordinary language. This leaves no room for the philosopher's search for a ground. That search is shown to be both vain and unnecessary.

But philosophy it is not so easily dismissed. This time it is historical reflection that comes to the rescue of philosophy by reminding us that ordinary language can furnish at best a shifting ground and, more importantly, by preventing us from drawing a sharp distinction between ordinary language and the discourse of philosophers. Much of what has come to be established, accepted, and taken for granted today can be shown to have its origin in past philosophy. Our common sense has its roots in past metaphysics and becomes questionable as these roots are questioned. Only to the extent that we forget history can we find security in ordinary language.

But it is not necessary to turn to history to find the appeal to ordinary language questionable. Such language itself forces us to raise questions. Consider the language of our neighbors, of our mass media, or of our politicians. To understand it is to gain insight into a way of life. To accept it without question is indeed to know one's place and, knowing one's place, to know what is to be done. Consider an extreme example: the language of a statesman justifies what should be considered murder by calling it a patriotic duty.

In such cases, too, particular language-games reveal particular forms of life. Does this mean that the philosopher cannot criticize them? Are we stuck with, "Of course, we would call this murder, but they call it a patriotic deed"? Examples from distant and, unfortunately, all too recent history are easy to find. Or should we perhaps deny that these are good examples of ordinary language? Consider the special vocabulary introduced by the Nazis to cover up the criminality of their actions. Of course, when the matter is phrased this way we are already saying that the Nazis had something to hide; the language that they were inventing was precisely language invented to cover up something. But are we not taking the superiority of our point of view for granted here? After all, the language-games played by the Nazis did not constitute an idling of language. Such language use did constitute an integral "part of an activity, a form of life," even if we feel that we must reject it. Many a good Nazi thought he was merely doing his duty, while we would like to insist that his duty lay in quite another place. To accept ordinary language as a ground is to admit that such feelings cannot be justified to one who happens to be playing a different language-game.

In the case of Wittgenstein it was perhaps his one-sided choice of examples that led him to overlook how questionable ordinary language can be. Thus he neglects the whole area of decision and choice. What is distinctive about this area is that here the future presents itself most insistently in its openness. Take the problem of abortion. Is abortion murder? Ordinary language here no longer offers us a secure ground; it fails to

31

provide an unambiguous answer to this question, partly because the meaning of what it is to be a person has become unclear: what defines human existence? Where does it begin and where does it end?

Responsibility demands that we not simply follow established practice, but that we help to shape it. If such shaping is not to be arbitrary, it must be coupled with a critical assessment of what is usually taken for granted. Because man faces an open future, the question, "What is man's place?" is one he will never be done with. The dislocation in which philosophy has its origin is nothing other than freedom itself. The attempt to present ordinary language as a ground is born of a dread of freedom, which lets the individual seek refuge in the established and accepted. What one says and does takes care of decision while the insecurity that is inseparable from the human situation is covered up. The philosopher's turn to ordinary language is a turn to inauthenticity.

This of course is not to deny that it is often quite useful to bring words back from their metaphysical to their everyday use. Wittgenstein was quite right to insist that there is something terribly artificial about many of the traditional problems of philosophy. But the history of philosophy can hardly be reduced to a history of such pseudoproblems. Was Socrates not right to question Euthyphro's use of "piety," Laches' use of "courage," Thrasymachus' use of "justice"? Must we not question an Eichmann's use of "duty"? Or is it simply a matter of expressing societal preferences? When we look at everyday language in all its variety—and the conversations of our neighbors or what we find in a newspaper will be a better guide to it than the examples offered by philosophers—do we really recognize here a ground we can trust, or do we discover that what we find is in need of questioning? Wittgenstein is quite right when he suggests that philosophical problems seem to say "I don't know my way about." But such dislocation is inseparable from decision. To face a decision is not yet to have made up one's mind. As long as we are engaged in the world, following a prescribed route, we may be able to avoid asking such questions, at least as long as nothing happens that throws us off our path. We raise questions when life releases us for a moment, when we are on a holiday, free from the demands of everyday. We also raise questions when some event shatters what we thought had been securely established. Freedom requires that there be a distance between the person and established and accepted norms that renders them questionable and in need of justification.

If philosophy has its origin in dislocation, it is an attempt at relocation. Thus it is more than idle curiosity. The fundamental question of philosophy is: where is man's place? Philosophy remains alive only as long as this question continues to be asked, because that place remains questionable and man's vocation remains ambiguous. It comes to an end when such questioning ceases, either because that place is taken to have been established or because the philosopher's search is thought to be an impossible one.

IV

There is a widespread feeling today that philosophy may have outlived itself, that the philosopher's work makes no difference to the society in which he lives. And the philosopher, far from disputing the irrelevance of his work, may even glory in it and insist once again that the dignity of philosophy is inseparable from its uselessness. Viewed in this manner philosophy becomes, like other expressions of curiosity, an escape from the burdens of everyday life, a game, a usually harmless diversion. One only wonders why society should think it important to support such inquiry.

That philosophy can have a different function is shown by that hostility which led the Athenians to condemn Socrates to death. Socrates was accused as an evil-doer who corrupted the young and did not believe in the gods of the state, but who believed instead in his own divinities. Both charges had their point. The deity who called Socrates to his life of questioning did not belong with the public gods, who appear to give supernatural blessing to what is being done. Having been called away from the usually taken for granted, Socrates called on others to think for themselves. Established society recognized and dealt with the threat that this posed by condemning Socrates to death, thus demonstrating its own weakness.

Even if it will find a genuinely critical philosophy troublesome, a healthy society must allow for places where presuppositions and commitments, established ways of seeing and thinking, are challenged. Without such challenge, what has come to be taken for granted is likely to be mistaken for what *has* to

33

be. Without that challenge, the past will suffocate the future. Philosophy should be such a place of challenge. Its point is not to entertain, nor is it to comfort. Philosophy should make us uncomfortable, and if it is to do so, if it is to lead us beyond the boundaries of common sense, we must make sure that the distance that separates the philosopher from the public is preserved. A society possessing the courage to face change and the willingness to assume responsibility for an uncertain future will support philosophy, knowing that often the return for such support will be questions and provocations.

Such a defense of the critical function of philosophy presupposes that criticism can lead to a better determination of the place where we should stand. Someone who lacked the confidence that philosophy can help to determine that place would have to consider the philosopher's insistence on criticism destructive. Do we still have that confidence? Philosophers like Wittgenstein or Heidegger, but more importantly the shape of the world we live in, have made it difficult not to feel that the search for norms and essences rests on a vain hope for a final security that reflects, rather than cures, our sense of dislocation. And indeed, the philosopher's flight beyond the earth has not yielded and cannot yield norms that can guide us. Uncertain of itself, sensing that it has lost its way, philosophy turns into metaphilosophical speculation on the place of philosophy.

If the society into which this self-questioning philosophy belongs were itself sure of man's place, one could perhaps welcome the loss of a genuinely critical philosophy. But the loss of way in which philosophy has its origin is not only still with us; it has been raised to a higher power and has become a determining structure of our culture, shaped as that culture is by science. For science is an offspring of philosophy. It presupposes the philosopher's flight beyond the particular and concrete and the commitment to objectivity made possible by that flight.[12] But that commitment is inseparable from a loss of place. The questionable and ambiguous character of science has become increasingly apparent: on one hand, we cannot deny that it has brought us mastery over nature and even over our own selves; on the other hand, it has increased the sense of the contingency and arbitrariness of our lives. Technology, the revolution in communications, and increased mobility have made the often-resented accidents of birth, sex, and location far less a destiny

34

that the individual has to accept. They promise realization of age-old dreams of personal autonomy. But these dreams are shadowed by the specter of a rootlessness that threatens to deny us any sense of place, vocation, and meaning. Science is linked with nihilism by the ontology of objectivity on which both depend. This gives new urgency to the question, "What is man's place?"

The need for philosophy remains thus very much alive. But since the philosopher's traditional commitment to objectivity and to theoretical inquiry is part of the problem, what is needed is a philosophy that includes a critical reflection on itself. Such reflection will have to center on the ideal of objectivity. While we cannot deny the legitimacy of this ideal, we also have to recognize that it can never be fully realized, that all our descriptions and prescriptions have their foundation in a creative interpretation of what more immediately presents itself and claims us. All the language-games that shape our experience and thought have historical roots; they are the work of our predecessors, work that is necessarily lacking in finality and therefore questionable, in need of critical appropriation. This is also true of the language of philosophy. It, too, demands to be questioned and such questioning will remain superficial as long as it is not tied to historical reflection. Philosophy becomes rootless and uncritical without the history of philosophy.

Philosophy also cannot be separated from the attempt to gain a philosophical understanding of history. One thing philosophy can still learn from the Marxists is to take history, and not only the history of philosophy, seriously. Only a philosophy that allies itself with history can hope to exhibit the presuppositions that determine our culture. Only in uncovering these presuppositions do we gain that distance from them which is a necessary condition of critical evaluation. We learn that the path which our culture took was not the only one that could have been taken. In the past one can find hints of alternatives that are desperately needed. Just in passing I would like to point to the Renaissance, to the fifteenth and sixteenth centuries, as to a period in which decisions were made whose impact remains to be fully understood.

But our consideration of history would be blind if it were not illuminated by a sense of what is right and wrong with that place we happen to find ourselves in. History must be joined to critical reflection. But once again we have to ask: Where do we find the necessary criteria? The attempt to discover such criteria would be hopeless if our understanding of reality were circumscribed by that modern world which has its dominant theme in science and technology. But the world we live in is not so one-dimensional. Even if science and technology have decisively shaped it, they are not its only theme. There are other dimensions to which we can open ourselves that reach back further in time. Here, too, history can assist criticism. Nietzsche's *Birth of Tragedy* points in this direction and in spite of its youthful carelessness it provides a needed model.

But we cannot sacrifice the future to the past. The turn to the past that has constituted the present and that thus helps determine the range of future possibilities is indeed necessary to make criticism responsible and not merely utopian. History limits the kind of answer that can be given to the question: "What is our place?" At the same time, history may help us to open ourselves to claims that need to be acknowledged, even if the shape of our world may make such acknowledgment difficult. But just as the past may help us to recognize our vocation, it can also stand in the way of a creative response to what now speaks to us and to what awaits us. We cannot simply use the maps of the past to establish where we should stand in the future. Our changed situation requires new maps. To furnish such maps is what I want to call the poetic function of philosophy. With it we come to what makes philosophy both most questionable and most exciting. Nietzsche's *Zarathustra* can serve as an illustration.

This poetic function, if it is to yield more than mere poetry, must not only remain open to what more immediately claims and moves those whom it would address; it also must remain rooted in a common history so that what it establishes can be received as an interpretation of the community's inherited destiny. Still, there cannot be already established criteria that will enable us in the end to judge such creative establishment. All genuine creative work must push beyond common sense. It may therefore be easy for those who don't recognize in such poetic philosophy an articulation of their own vocation to dismiss it as mere poetry or perhaps as nonsense. Nevertheless, if there are no longer philosophers who have the courage and strength to become poets in this sense, philosophy is dead and belongs in a

36

museum. Nietzsche can serve as a test case. Does he belong in a museum? Or can we take him seriously as he took Schopenhauer seriously, not so much for what he thought—although here, too, there is still a great deal that remains to be thought through and appropriated—but for the example he set, as an educator.

Notes

1. Compare with Gottlob Frege, "The Thought; A Logical Inquiry," trans. A. M. and M. Quinton, in *Essays on Frege,* ed. E. D. Klemke (Urbana, Illinois: University of Illinois Press, 1968), p. 515: "The more exactly scientific an exposition is the less will the nationality of its author be discernible and the easier will it be to translate. On the other hand, the constituents of language, to which I want to call attention here, make the translation of poetry very difficult, even make a complete translation almost always impossible, for it is in precisely that in which poetic value consists that languages differ most."

2. Ibid., p. 511.

3. Ibid., p. 519, fn.

4. Descartes, *Discourse on Method,* in *Philosophical Works,* vol. 1, pt. 1, trans. Elizabeth S. Haldane and G. R. T. Ross (New York: Dover, 1955), p. 86.

5. Aristotle *Metaphysics* I, 2; 982 b., trans. W. D. Ross.

6. Plato *Theaetetus* 1973 E., trans. B. Jowett.

7. Aristotle *Metaphysics* I, 2; 982 b.

8. Martin Heidegger, *Sein und Zeit,* 7th ed. (Tübingen: Niemeyer, 1953), p. 229; and his *Being and Time,* trans. John Macquarrie and Edward Robinson (New York: Harper and Row, 1962), p. 272.

9. Augustine *The Confessions,* Book X, trans. E. B. Pusey (New York: Modern Library, 1949), p. 232.

10. Wittgenstein *Philosophical Investigations,* 123, trans. G. E. M. Anscombe.

11. Ibid., 7, 38, 132.

12. Compare with Karsten Harries, "Descartes Perspective, and the Angelic Eye," *Yale French Studies,* no. 49 (1973), pp. 28–42; and his "The Infinite Sphere: Comments on the History of a Metaphor," *The Journal of the History of Philosophy,* 13 (January 1975):5–15.

A Historical
Hypothesis

E. H. Gombrich

The question which was put to us was "Does history constitute a legitimate critical tool for the art or literary critic?"
There is a venerable philosophical teaser asking how many
grains of sand make a heap. I have been tempted to ask how
many minutes, days, years, or centuries turn an event into history. For me, history is simply a record of events; the invitation
to answer this question I received from Provo is no more or less
history than was the discovery of America, though admittedly it
may interest fewer people.

The record of events constituting history must always be in-
complete and selective. The principle of selection is called interest. Someone wants to know what happened, and he tries to
find out. There may be any number of motivations for wanting
to know, and there are any number of historical questions also
in the study of literature or of art. You may want to write the
history of the phrase "once upon a time." I don't know if that
has been done. Or you may want to plan a history of the greet-
ing card industry. Some of these histories are unlikely to be rele-

vant to art criticism; others may be. For art criticism creates its own history, not vice versa.

One thing is sure in my mind. If history is a record of events, events must take their course. Instant history, the recording only of the here and now, is not possible, because we have no means of telling what occurrence may or may not have consequences and, as a result, which ones might turn into significant events. Advertisers and promoters always pretend they know that this is a 'unique offer' and an 'unprecedented' historical event, but that is sheer bluffing. For the literary form of history is the narrative and the subject of the narrative is a 'story,' the sequence of coherent events.

For instance, there is a well-known store in London called Marks and Spencer. It plays a certain role in the economic history of the retail trade of England and one could certainly write its history either as a monograph or in a larger context. This history would have to begin with the meeting of a Mr. Marks and a Mr. Spencer and their decision, sudden or gradual, to form a partnership. But the first meeting of these two gentlemen only turned into history by hindsight. We now know that it had consequences. Not every meeting of two businessmen belongs to history in the sense that it can form the beginning of a narrative.

In the light of this example, there must be a difference, at least of degree, between art journalism and art criticism. The journalist must tell his readers that there is a show at a certain gallery and what kinds of things they may see there. He has every right also to tell them, "I like this stuff, and I hope you will also like it." But of the critic we expect a little more.

There are many critical terms that imply a historical judgment. The most obvious are those that relate to originality or its opposite, calling the work *bold, revolutionary, tame, eclectic, uninventive,* or *experimental.* All are related to comparisons with other works known to the critic and, presumably, to the author or artist. We tend to see the new work against the background of history, even if it is only the history of a recent movement, such as "op" art. Within a civilization that values innovation and creativity, however you wish to define or value these matters yourself, any work of art may be seen as a "move," a "decision," a choice between alternatives or the invention or discovery of fresh ones not known before. Thus even what is described as the ex-

40

pressive value of the work of art, its physiognomic character of severity or indulgence, mockery or solemnity cannot be judged outside the matrix of the situation within which it took shape. In other words, it cannot be judged without history. This is the point for which Professor Beardsley also referred to my view.

It is indeed possible to argue that the situation has got somewhat out of hand, that works of art are now too much judged as gestures rather than as things in themselves. In other words, we have a certain hypertrophic growth of historical awareness, or self-awareness, that has emptied the work of art of its intrinsic meaning. I believe that this is a defensible point of view; at any rate, it demonstrates the difference between the approach of a critic in this century and that of a patron in more stable societies not yet corroded by so much self-consciousness, who is watching for what others did, or do.

But even within the somewhat healthier framework of a somewhat more stable matrix, the critic cannot but measure the work against other works. The term *critic* means something like *discriminator,* a person who notices differences and who makes decisions about them. A work in total isolation could be enjoyed, but it could not be criticized, because there is nothing to compare it with.

It has been just one week since I entered the Church of Notre Dame in Paris and saw there, to my surprise—thinking of the present symposium—that the authorities of that great church in Paris believe in the value of historical comparison. As you enter there is a large display of photographs and notices showing the evolution of the Gothic cathedral in France. You see there ground plans and elevations, and photographs of six cathedrals: Saint Denis in 1140; Rouen in 1150; Notre Dame of Paris (where you stand) in 1163; Bouvais in 1185; Rheims in 1210; and Amiens in 1220. When you have seen the Church of Notre Dame in this context, as a link in the great story of the development of these tremendous buildings, you undeniably gain an extra dimension in your appreciation, though I would be the last to say that you cannot enjoy Notre Dame without knowing the ground plan of Saint Denis or of Amiens. But clearly there is a desire among visitors to put the work into its wider historical context to realize what the term "cathedral" means (*a Bishop's church*). If you thought of a cathedral as a modern building for exhibition or for the playing of games, it would look entirely different.

The historical and human context in which the church took shape cannot be eliminated from your response to that church, and here the problem of "problem-solutions" that Professor Beardsley mentioned, of course, also plays a part. The development of the cathedral is, among other things, a development of the ideal solution for this type of building, and historians, rightly or wrongly, speak also of the decadence of the cathedral as other concerns came in.

I am not out to defend this purely historical approach, but I am saying that it is very hard to see how we could get along entirely without it, imagining ourselves as totally innocent visitors from Mars suddenly confronted with a structure of this kind. But as I argued in the Romanes Lecture on "Art History and Social Sciences" given at Oxford, discrimination—whether in food, in sports, in dress, in ice skating, in ballet, in acting, in writing, in singing, in painting, or in any other activity—develops within a circle of what one might call "fans," lovers of a particular activity, who argue among themselves about excellence and about the dimensions of the particular hobby or art. These are the critics; their criticism, no doubt, is linked to history insofar as it is rooted in comparisons and in experience. Standards emerge; once in a while a new contribution sets an entirely fresh standard. Perhaps one did not know before Casals that the cello could sound like he made it sound.

It is not indispensable for such standards to be systematically recorded or remembered. One can be convinced that Garrick was a great actor and made a difference to the history of the stage, even though one realizes that his performances are beyond recall. Here historians report to the critic about events that resulted in that final effect of art and literature, the effect of admiration. In praising a new work, the critic makes a bid for admiration. He wants to enlist the work in the company of masterpieces, to range it in what I have called the canon. He even wants to claim that art itself will be affected by this new work, and that this new work will one day be part of history in that valuative sense. However much that claim is often abused, it does make sense when it is expressed as a hypothesis, a historical hypothesis.

Literary
History and
Literary Criticism

René Wellek

I address myself to the question asked in the very beginning: "Does history constitute a legitimate critical tool for art criticism?" As a literary critic, I shall think of the criticism of literature in particular.

First, it seems to me that one cannot possibly escape history in discussing literature. As an example, read the first lines of Ariosto's *Orlando Furioso,* in which the poet announces that he will "sing of ladies and knights." Unless you know what a lady is and what a knight is (and this is by no means obvious today), you will not fully understand even the first line of the poem. The meaning of lady and knight is already a historical question. The same is true of many of our words: they are embedded in history. Some historical knowledge is required to understand them properly. A person totally unacquainted with Western civilization could not properly read and understand a work by Ariosto and Dante. There is no doubt that the historical meaning of words is necessary to a full understanding of most literature.

There is also another obvious use of history for literary study:

many references in a work are often incomprehensible unless you know the historical circumstances to which they allude. There is an enormous literature commenting on the *Divine Comedy* of Dante that explains all the allusions. In many places we cannot understand the text fully unless we know to what Dante was referring.

History thus elucidates literature. Many works of art, even very recent ones, cannot be understood without history. Thus many poems by Yeats remain obscure unless one knows something about the Irish rebellion in 1916. To understand Andrew Marvell's "Horatian Ode" you have to know something of Cromwell's conquest of Ireland and King Charles I's execution in London and something about the political situation in the summer of 1650.

Nobody, I conclude, can doubt the explanatory value of history for literature. But does history matter for the criticism, the judging of literature? The point was made by Professor Gombrich when he spoke of the question of originality. The originality, the novelty of a work of art is an issue in all critical discussion and there the daily critic—the journalist—often shows his ignorance and would profit from historical knowledge that would allow him to recognize the model of a given work.

I can support this idea with an example from my own experience. I remember when, as a youngster, I read Pearl Buck's *The Good Earth*. I liked the book and admired it. But when I later read Knut Hamsun's *The Growth of the Soil* I discovered that *The Good Earth* was an imitation of Hamsun's book. Pearl Buck transferred the setting from the Norwegian peasantry to China. Even the pseudo-Biblical style is extremely similar. When I discovered that *The Good Earth* is an imitation, my attitude and even my value judgment toward the work changed. Thus the question of originality, of novelty becomes very important for the study of literature. I would say that a work of literature must be seen in the context of a genre tradition, and in the tradition of literature in general. You may go astray unless you see it within the whole literary tradition.

Literary history in itself is a subject of enormous scope and interest that has engaged many minds for centuries. I have just now defended its importance. But I admit that literary history can also become dangerous to a proper understanding of literature. It can obscure the aesthetic judgment, its background in-

44

formation can overwhelm and smother the work of art under a mound of learning that is brought in from all ends and corners.

Take, for instance, a work such as the *Dunciad* of Alexander Pope that requires a lot of historical explanation. The *Dunciad* contains hundreds of allusions to writers who are totally unknown today. There is a fine edition by an eminent scholar, James Sutherland, which has elaborate notes that identify every one of these Grub Street authors and that tell their history. When Pope wrote the *Dunciad* he probably knew only a fraction of the annotation contents that appear in Mr. Sutherland's edition. On the other hand, one can read the *Dunciad* as a satire and see all those names as swarms of insects buzzing around. You just note them as names—comic and repulsive names—and you don't need to know when the authors attacked were born or what they wrote, and so on.

It seems to me that our immediate relation to a work of art can be blunted by an excessive amount of historical information. There is a point where history fails. It cannot determine quality. I agree with what Mr. Beardsley quoted from Jakob Rosenberg. I think we, however, can recognize quality better if we have experience in judging works of art, in comparing and grading them.

We thus come to the difficult problems of originality and the question of fakes and forgeries that has been discussed at length in art history, such as the fake Vermeers painted by Jan Van Meegeren. Harkness Tower on the campus of Yale University is an exact replica of the *Tour de Beurre* in Rouen. Is it, we may ask, as valuable as the original work? Though it is a fake, let us assume that the reproduction is absolutely exact. There is an argument against imitation, even if the imitation is perfect.

One danger of the historical approach is what has been called "historicism." I use the term not in the sense of Karl Popper's *Poverty of Historicism* where it means theories of history (like those of Hegel and Marx) that predict the future, but I use it in the more widely accepted sense as historical relativism, the feeling that everything is relative in its time and place, and that we should appreciate with total sympathy everything that existed in history.

There is a well-known quotation originally ascribed to Leibniz and repeated by Johan Gottfried Herder, one of the founders of the historicist point of view. He said something like this: "I like every book I have read. I never read anything I disliked." Herder recommends the "natural method" or criticism which, he says, "leaves every flower in its place, and contemplates it just as it is, according to time and kind, from the root to the crown. Lichen, moss, fern and the richest scented flower each blooms in its place in God's order." I think this, however, is an error. Works of art are not works of God. Works of art are made by man, and therefore they are criticizable. They can be changed, improved, and condemned, while we cannot really criticize the crocodile or snail or cucumber. But we *can* criticize works of literature.

I think the view that says we must like everything and that we must justify everything in its historical place is obfuscating. It leads to complete skepticism, to indifference. It is one of the troubles with the humanities. The lawyer knows what is right and wrong, or at least he pretends he knows or thinks that he knows. The physician knows what is healthy or what is unhealthy, or at least he thinks he knows. The scientist knows the truth, knows what is real and what is false. But the humanist, or the student of literature, says often, "I don't know. I can't say why this is greater than that." It is a failure of the humanist that he cannot stand up for his convictions, cannot distinguish between good and bad art, good and bad literature.

The literary historian, to my mind, needs criticism more often than the critic needs literary history. The literary historian cannot judge, cannot decide what is important, what is unimportant unless he is a critic. He has to make choices all the time. There is a constant process of evaluation going on. We have millions of books, and out of these millions of books the literary historian and the critic chooses a very small selection, and even from this small selection he has to choose the traits he is going to discuss. There may be hundreds and even thousands of these traits in a single work of art. The critic, of course, should also know literary history because he would be cut off from the past if he were ignorant of it. Professor Harries has made an eloquent plea for the importance of the history of philosophy for philosophy. The same is true in literary criticism. It needs literary history in the sense of a knowledge of the past, or a sense of the present growing out of the past. Literary history can be decisive for the solution of many critical and theoretical problems today.

The Well-Read
Urn: A
Thought Experiment

E. D. Hirsch, Jr.

So far I detect so much agreement among those of us who are supposed to disagree with each other that I think my paper may be a fictional work, really, in which I am inventing a disagreement.

The question, "How much attention should we pay to history in the criticism of art?" is, I would say, a nontheoretical question, and is, instead, as Professor Wellek clearly put it, an ethical question. A lot of critical theory tells us that art has such and such a character, not because that theory is a disinterested description of the case, but because that is the way the theorist wants us to regard art. If we are told, for instance, that it is the nature of art to be purposeless (the famous formulation of Kant), then the definition, the "theoretical" definition, becomes a secret imperative that says: "When you meet a so-called work of art, you ought to regard it with a disinterested contemplation of its form, telling us what is better form, and what is worse form, as in the quotation from Rosenberg that Professor Beardsley read. That is the proper approach to art because it corresponds to the nature of art."

But the theoretical statement in this case is not a description at all, but rather a moral injunction that has no necessary relation to what we call art. And, similarly, I think, theories that tell us we ought to pay attention to the historical context of an art work may have no more purely theoretical justification than those theories that tell us to disregard historical context in favor of a truly aesthetic approach. The theoretical pretensions of these imperatives could be as ill-founded on the historical side as they are on the nonhistorical side. They don't derive, as they pretend, from the nature of art, but come instead from some ethical preference about art, or some preference about the way to interpret art, that the theorist wants us to share with him.

So, having said this much, I won't be misunderstood when I make the following observations about history and criticism; nobody will think I am trying to ground what I say in pure description, or logic, or the nature of art. If I favor a historical approach, my disagreement with aesthetic or existential views will not be a theoretical disagreement, but a practical disagreement about some concrete and practical matters.

My further claim is that injunctions to disregard historical context (I haven't heard such injunctions here, I may say), whatever their elaborate theoretical justifications, will often lead to practical embarrassments, and also to offenses against common sense.

Take a concrete example: Keats's *Ode on a Grecian Urn*. It is a poem that everybody knows, and almost everybody admires. So it is a convenient subject for a thought experiment that I'll invite you to make in order to see what happens when the two different imperatives about history are followed out to their logical or ideological conclusion. In the one case we are enjoined to ignore the historical context and regard Keats's poem as a poem. On the other side, we are asked by the historicists to reconstruct the original context and determine the author's original intention.

The special convenience of the Keats poem for this experiment is the actual existence of an anthology that contains several dozen commentaries on Keats's poem. This collection is, of course, called *The Well-Read Urn*. It contains at least forty commentaries on the last lines of the poem. These are the lines (you know them):

> *"Beauty is truth, truth beauty, that is all*
> *Ye know on earth, and all ye need to know."*

In the several dozen commentaries, we can discover about four quite disparate interpretations of those lines. I won't explain in detail what the four disparate interpretations are, since that's not really germane to the thought experiment and it might even distract us. But I will mention just one of the comments, one by T. S. Eliot. I don't know if I am quoting him precisely, but he says something like this: "Either I do not understand those lines, or they state something which is untrue."

Let us suppose that the four disparate interpretations of the lines are the only meanings, now, that readers construe, and let's also suppose that they are all equally plausible and satisfactory from an aesthetic standpoint. The aesthetic or existential theorists would tell us that all four interpretations should be accepted; never mind the original historical context or motivation. I think I would agree—and perhaps you will, too, under the circumstances that I have just described—that the aesthetic or the existential theorist would have a point. Nobody knows what Keats meant anyway, and so we have no basis for resisting the tolerant injunction to live and let live.

But I want to carry the thought experiment one stage further. Let there appear on the scene a scholar-critic of great authority, a combination of Kittredge and Trilling, with the following sensational announcement: he has discovered a new Keats letter explaining exactly what Keats meant to convey by the lines at the end of his poem. Our great critic will also explain that this is one of the four extant readings, and it is not only what Keats meant, but it is also a very profound and compelling meaning for the poem. Our imagined critic is so famous that his scholarly pronouncement is widely promulgated in the schools and colleges; it even makes the front pages of the newspapers. Nobody seriously doubts anymore that Keats's meaning is established.

Now, I'd like to predict what the practical result of this thought experiment would be. The aesthetic or existential critic will assert that all four readings continue to be valid, and we must not be misled by the supposed reconstructions of supposed historical intentions. Keats has no exclusive ownership of the lines after he put them forward in the world; they belong to the English language. We know what the words "beauty," "truth," and "That is all you need to know" mean. There is no problem of archeological reconstruction here; it is the duty of the critic to remake meanings anyway.

Nevertheless, my prediction is that these theoretical urgings will no longer have very much practical effect; it is too late. The lines have now been placed in a different cultural category than they occupied before, and they will find themselves alongside that great army of verses that everybody understands: "A little learning is a dangerous thing"; "To be or not to be, that is the question"; "The boy stood on the burning deck"; and "After many a summer dies the swan." So at this point the theoretical and ideological conflict no longer has any practical consequences.

This seems to suggest that theoretical arguments about history occur mainly when there is some serious doubt about what a poem means or when there is a theoretical debate between theorists at a symposium of this kind. The supposedly momentous issue becomes a real issue only in those concrete cases where our historical knowledge is very insecure, which, of course, is most of the time. But the concession still doesn't speak to the result of my thought experiment. It therefore seems to me that the best recourse of the theorist who prefers historical reconstruction (I place myself on that side) is, of *course,* to make the best arguments he can in the theoretical domain, but also to place very little reliance on such pseudotheoretical issues. The best strategy of the historicist-critic is probably to encourage and pursue good history.

History as a
Critical Tool:
A Dialogue

BEARDSLEY: Just to generate some discussion here, I'll ask
René Wellek about his experience with Pearl Buck's novel, *The
Good Earth,* and the disappointment that came from discovering
later that *The Good Earth* is but a feeble imitation of another
novel of the same genre by Knut Hamsun. (The books may not
have stemmed from exactly the same genre, but they are the
same kind of novel.)

René Wellek, somewhat uncharacteristically in this case but
perhaps just out of an attempt to see both sides of the question,
said that when he discovered that the book was an imitation, he
concluded that the novel was less good than he had originally
thought. I want to question this conclusion. The book is just as
good as it ever was, and the fact that it is an imitation of a better novel doesn't make it a worse novel. In fact, if it is a good
imitation of a good novel, it might even be a miracle, so I don't
quite see why one lowers one's judgment of it by virtue of this
discovery.

WELLEK: I think it is only a comparative judgment. I became aware of something better.

BEARDSLEY: Then that's all right. The new judgment is based on a comparison with the Hamsun novel. You are not saying that *The Good Earth* is worse than you thought it was; you are only saying that you now see something better—Hamsun's novel.

WELLEK: Or I am saying that I introduced a new criterion, a historical criterion, which I had not been able to use or had not been interested in using before. I discovered, through historical comparison, that *The Good Earth* is an imitation. This may be a criterion irrelevant to immediate aesthetic contemplation, but I think it is relevant to any attempt to put the book into a historical context.

HARRIES: Perhaps one can give a bit more focus to this discussion by picking up a word you use: *novelty*. That is, to what extent are we prepared to grant novelty a status in assessing the merits of a work of art? As an extreme example, take Duchamp's notorious urinal. Suppose I read about this and interpreted it as an invitation to take all sorts of bathroom fixtures to the museum. Obviously in this extreme case, where the aesthetic effect has been almost reduced to that of making a novel statement, it is quite clear that the repetition is worthless. Professor Wellek, seeing my bathtub for the first time, might call it "a startling statement." But then he sees the Duchamp. My statement would be totally undercut by this subsequent discovery.

WELLEK: I would recognize that novelty is not in itself a decisive criterion. There is also original rubbish.

HARRIES: But you would grant it some status.

WELLEK: That's right.

GOMBRICH: But I wouldn't grant it any. If I may be really controversial, I think the glorification of this kind of a schoolboy joke and the role it has become in debates about art is one of the most degrading things that has happened to art since its very beginning—even since the cave man! I am not condemning Duchamp for making a joke, but I am condemning all of us for talking about it after so many years, and for being so solemn about it, and for making it into a new definition of art. Unfortunately, I have read a good deal about it. I feel ashamed that I have read so much about it because, after all, it is only the commentary of the so-called art world that has made this into such an event. In all European cities at the time of carnival there were artists' fêtes in which jokes of this kind flourished; happily, they were enjoyed only for a moment and then they were forgotten. Making a joke like Duchamp's urinal a turning point in the history of art is most puzzling. I wonder how this should be possible.

HARRIES: But we shouldn't be quite so startled by all this. Duchamp offers us, in a way, a caricature of a very important tradition that began with Friedrich Schlegel's notion of the interesting. I, like you, would criticize this tradition. But I think we have to see this tradition as a really important part, in a broad sense, of aesthetic activity in the nineteenth and twentieth centuries. We can't just dismiss Duchamp as an isolated instance here. He just caricatures an important tendency.

WELLEK: You can use the example of John Cage's piece of music in which a performer appeared at the piano for exactly three minutes and forty-four seconds and did nothing at all. I remember I got an angry letter from Richard Kostelanetz chiding me for not appreciating the profound significance of this "music of silence."

GOMBRICH: It is a talking point.

WELLEK: Actually, a pantomime that is supposed to surprise and shock you was being performed. The shock effect of art is, I think, much older than Friedrich Schlegel. It occurs in the Baroque: "Meraviglia" was a theoretical demand in Baroque poetics. But things have now gotten out of hand. People have to do something new at any price, so they try to think of something absolutely unheard of—something outrageous.

GOMBRICH: But I wish those people had better ideas.

HIRSCH: I want to return to the original point from which the Duchamp digression departed: the significance of novelty and the difference it makes to what you might call a correct or true aesthetic evaluation.

There is a passage in one of Emil Staiger's critical books where he confesses that he had thought a particular love song was a bad love poem, that it belonged to the nineteenth century and was merely a sentimental fake version of an earlier, more genuine tradition. But when he later realized that he had made a historical mistake, he had a different conception of the quality

53

of the poem. He thought it was a much better poem than before—just the reverse of Professor Wellek's experience. These experiences exist. There needs to be some explanation for them, and I don't think all that happened in them was that the copy just *seemed* to be inferior. I think, in agreement with the historicist's argument, that there is a dimension beyond the formal character of the art work as you see it physically before you. There is a spiritual dimension to it that is not in the physical manifestation. That spiritual dimension is of utmost significance, and no amount of perfection of style alone, or of stylistic manipulation alone, can reach that dimension. It is the discovery of mind or spirit in a communication between persons that adds that further dimension, that something which is to me the greatest significance found in art, and does not just keep within the formal boundaries of the vehicle itself. So I think the example of novelty is a rather significant example of why history is really important in understanding a work of art, even in aesthetic terms.

GOMBRICH: Consider forgery, which is so often used to show that people are taken in by names, and to demonstrate that people like a work of art because, seeing the name, they think it is better: they like a painting as long as they think it is by Vermeer, and when it turns out to be by Van Meegeren, they no longer like it. But first of all, there is a mind behind it. Van Meegeren was a crook and a madman; one doesn't like the feeling of having been deceived, but there is again the question of the context in which the famous painting by this forger was made. After all, if you want to make another thought experiment, imagine that this painting by the forger Van Meegeren had been found in the caves of Lascaux and that there was absolute, inescapable, certain evidence that it was painted about 20,000 years before Christ. In every respect that painting would be a miracle. We would have to revise our whole idea about the human mind and about human history. It would be an example of prophecy. It would be something absolutely incredible. So to say that it doesn't matter when the painting was done (which, of course, you didn't say) seems to me to run the danger of absurdity.

BEARDSLEY: That seems to be very just and legitimate.

HARRIES: Let me lead this discussion in a somewhat different direction. It seems obvious to me that to read a poem in another language, we first have to learn that language. The question is, how far can that notion be—or should that notion be—meaningfully expanded? For instance, the Ariosto example did something like expand that notion of language towards knights—in this case to understand the work of art we also have to know something about knights. That seems obvious. Here it still seems quite innocent. But how far should we go in the visual arts? Take, for instance, a church. In appreciating this architecture, do we appreciate it as a church? Are there two kinds of responses, first to an abstracted sort of pure architecture, which then also happens to be a church? I would argue that to appreciate this building is to appreciate it as a solution to a particular problem: the building of a church. And if we don't know what a church is, then we don't know the language of this art. And so in the end the turn to history is, I think, absolutely essential to acquire the language that allows us to understand a particular work of art. I think this works for the visual arts just as much as it does for literature where it has its first home.

GOMBRICH: I always like to be as concrete as possible, and sitting here with these paintings on the wall, I have a question. I know enough to know what a covered wagon is, and I do understand a great deal about this painting here. I am not quite sure that I understand what is represented in the other painting. It certainly does affect me.

WELLEK: You wouldn't understand it unless you knew about it—it is the seagulls.

GOMBRICH: I see seagulls, all right.

WELLEK: They ate the crickets.

HARRIES: You've been enlightened now: it's in remembrance of an incident in Mormon history.

WELLEK: The seagulls devoured the crickets and saved the first Mormon harvest.

GOMBRICH: Well, you see, it is an important point of understanding that one must know the history.

HIRSCH: I couldn't understand it, either. I've been looking at it ever since I came in.

GOMBRICH: None of us can look at any painting without seeing it in some certain historical context. We recognize the style of the painting, and some of its other elements, when we enter the room. We make some sort of placement of this painting within the spectrum of possibility. Of course, as a historian I may be more biased in this respect, but I would say that any-body who is at all alive to art would see the style and the character of these paintings together with the subject.

BEARDSLEY: I wonder if you would agree with me on this distinction, though. There are two things we can say about what one of these paintings represents. We can say it depicts a cov-ered wagon—not any particular covered wagon, but just a cov-ered wagon—or we can say it represents a particular historical event. To know which historical event it portrays, we *do* have to know some specific history, but in order to know only that it de-picts a covered wagon, we *don't* have to know any specific his-tory: we only have to know that at some time or other there was such a thing as a covered wagon. We don't need to know any dates or any other historical information.

WELLEK: To an observer who knows no history, the paint-ing simply depicts a covered wagon against the mountains. But doesn't it represent the arrival of the covered wagons in Salt Lake City? It is quite a definite historical event that is depicted here.

BEARDSLEY: But, you see, I want to make a distinction and say that it portrays a particular historical event, but that it also depicts various objects, such as mountains. You don't have to know any history in order to recognize that it depicts a mountain. You don't have to know anything about when moun-tains were formed: all you have to know is that there are such things as mountains. That knowledge doesn't really involve his-tory.

HARRIES: Back to the language example: suppose you read a poem in German. If your German isn't very good, you might get a limited enjoyment from the poem. Similarly, one might discover a work of art where certain dimensions are indeed ac-cessible without one having to work terribly hard. In that case one would be in the position of a person who, not knowing the language very well, gets a certain minimal appreciation of the poem, but this is not to say that the dimensions of the poem that make it a great poem are really available.

GOMBRICH: I would like to refer briefly to one point in Professor Beardsley's paper. He rightly picks out the rather ab-struse example of Millard Meiss's ostrich egg as a marginal note, but what if a person doesn't know who the Holy Virgin is? That is also history. Or what the prayer gesture means? The prayer gesture is not something that everybody recognizes: it is something historical. It didn't even exist before the twelfth century in the West.

WELLEK: We come to a point where knowledge becomes irrelevant to the artistic judgment about the quality of a painting. This is true in reference to the ostrich eggs in the Piero della Francesca. There comes a point where this information, however important and interesting (for I *am* interested in iconography; however, these ostrich eggs surely can be discovered in totally unimportant paintings), has very little artistic value. It is important to understand iconography when you see the Piero della Francesca, but the Piero della Francesca simply has to be judged as a painting finally, having some kind of artistic quality that you cannot escape, and that I think in some way is an ahistorical judgment.

GOMBRICH: It is certainly an ahistorical judgment, but can it be entirely divorced from history? I am thinking now about the forger. Samuel Butler enjoyed composing like Handel; he thought Handel's way was the only correct way of writing music. But if we know that this is a pastiche of Handel from the late nineteenth century, it becomes something different, I would think. Perhaps we go a little too far in this, but there is a genuine problem, I think. If somebody were capable of painting the Brera altarpiece, which I doubt, it would still be something different if it had been done today.

HIRSCH: Going back to the covered wagon and the mountains: if I understand you right, Mr. Beardsley, you are saying we may decide there is a point beyond which we don't want to play the historical game anymore. It sounds as though there are moral imperatives involved. Some people are telling us we can't really see a picture at all unless we go quite far into history. You are saying, "No, I don't want to go that far." That seems to me a defensible position. But I think it must be understood that the issue is not a theoretical one. It is no more than a cultural imperative about the way we should deal with works of art.

BEARDSLEY: I am sympathetic with your suggestion, which I think is a very important methodological one. Some of these conflicts that initially seem conflicts might be translated into differences about what resolutions to make, what decisions to make. Suppose I look at a painting depicting some sort of a

57

tool. What sort of a tool is it? What is the tool used for? How do we recognize what is depicted in this painting, and what sort of knowledge does such recognition require? We recognize that the painting depicts human beings. We need some knowledge to see that the painting depicts human beings, but I don't think that knowledge is strictly historical knowledge. That knowledge depends on experience: we have to have seen human beings, or seen other pictures of them, or read stories about them that contained descriptions.

GOMBRICH: What about angels?

BEARDSLEY: That's why I included descriptive stories as a method of obtaining knowledge. We must have a verbal description of an angel, or we wouldn't recognize one when we saw it, which might be sooner than we think. I am really asking for the truth conditions for statements like "This painting depicts a dog." That doesn't involve a decision about how far I want to go, but it does involve an analysis of what we finally mean by the word *depicting*.

WELLEK: Going back to the question of novelty, I would agree that novelty is a very important criterion in the history of art. Taken in isolation in literature it would make the following judgment possible: Christopher Marlowe is more important than Shakespeare, because Marlowe was the innovator. But there is no doubt that on other grounds we would have to consider Shakespeare the far greater artist. So I think that innovation—novelty—in itself cannot be the final criterion of judgment.

BEARDSLEY: May I pursue another problem about the notion of communication? Communication is a word we use to talk about art. I think it's a tricky word. I'd like to distinguish between two different things that are involved in communication, and I'd like to reject one of them and accept the other. We say people are *communicating* with us when they can give us a message of some kind, when they say something to us. I agree that on such a basis many works of art can be called *communications*.

But there is another important dimension we sense when we look at works of art; this other dimension is a human context. Take as an example something that does not communicate by conveying a message. Listen to one of Mozart's string quintets, and you will understand the human dimension. It matters very much that I think of the string quartet as something that was made by a human being and as something that was made, in a way, for me (and for other people). Mozart has given us some of his own overflowing gifts; he has made something that he offers to other people, something very valuable, so there is communication in that sense. But that's not saying that in writing it he was trying to teach something or deliver a message.

I want to see if the same thing could be said of literary works to a certain extent. This brings me back to the example of the Keats poem. You predicted what would happen if a definitive letter was discovered in which Keats said explicitly what he meant by those last two mysterious and much-debated lines. But I'm afraid your prediction wouldn't apply to me in this case. I am more hard-boiled than that. I would instead be interested in what Keats *thought* he had succeeded in saying. I would then be glad to read the poem over again to see if indeed he had succeeded in saying what he intended. But at some point I might regretfully have to say that what he had intended to say wasn't in his poem. This often happens with poets. It doesn't happen too often with Keats, perhaps, but it happens with lesser poets.

And so I don't see why I should, at that point, close the books and simply say, "OK, that settles the question of what the poem means." It settles the question about what *Keats* meant, but that is not the same as settling the question about what the *poem* means. I still want to keep that distinction, if I can.

HIRSCH: This is an old song, and I just don't think that *poems* mean, but rather that *people* mean. When you are choosing, you choose a meaning that is different than Keats's quite deliberately, because you don't think his meaning fits the words as well as the meaning that you (and perhaps the rest of the public) will supply. In the experiment, that is why I wanted Keats's meaning to be one of the four meanings that people *have* seen in those last two lines, so you couldn't, under those conditions, say, "No, Keats didn't *succeed* in meaning that." People have, in fact, for many years now, accepted that as one of the meanings. The problem, then, is not what the *poem* means. I don't believe it makes sense to say that *words* mean anything by themselves; words are meaningful because of the way people understand them, or because of the way people meant them.

HARRIES: But Keats is not the only one here who understands these words. Suppose I want to paint something. I put

59

the first paint on the canvas. There it sits, an independent reality. Now, my project already has to be modified in view of that presence; similarly, when you try to write a poem, as soon as you put it down it becomes, in a sense, independent. You have to struggle with that line, or perhaps discard it—maybe it was not a good line. But when we speak of the meaning of the line, I don't think that is a private meaning, and that allows the point made. In other words, you don't need to give up your own interpretation.

HIRSCH: That's right. And I think that the common sense of the generality of men will take poetic language and non-poetic language in one dimension. If the question of what something means can be resolved in the way that I described it, then most people will go that way. There is a small cadre of theorists who take the other line. I'm saying there is one dimension in which people will take meanings in all literary characteristics to be at one with or in a continuum with all the other uses of language as they are meant by the person.

HARRIES: I would like to raise a question here about the line you used earlier, "To be, or not to be." I am not quite sure whether in the context that line is all that clear. In all the examples you gave me, once they appear in a literary work of art, they no longer seem so clear. You can't come up with an example that has the kind of clarity of "one plus one equals two."

HIRSCH: There are plenty of lines that are not discussed. In critical literature, we discuss the lines we don't understand. We don't very often spend a lot of time discussing works of literature we *do* understand. That is one of the reasons why *A Man for All Seasons* is not studied much I thought it was a very good modern play, and it has been a popular success, but it isn't studied in the higher reaches because it doesn't offer any problems of interpretation.

HARRIES: I wonder whether the fact that a text offers no problems of interpretation is the only reason why we don't study it. For instance, Brentano's poetry strikes me as an example of poetry that is terribly difficult to discuss because what happens is so subtle, depending, as it does, on consonance. It is obviously much less rewarding for the critic who wants an occasion for a brilliant piece of criticism than a poem by Blake or Hölderlin. Brentano's poetry doesn't lend itself to criticism in quite that way. Does that mean we really understand Brentano better than Hölderlin or Blake? Perhaps just the opposite is true. Perhaps his poetry is more mysterious.

Edmund Wilson
(1895-1972)

René Wellek

Edmund Wilson is the one American critic most widely known and read in Europe. In the United States he is (or rather was) a dominant figure: a man of letters, a general critic of society. Many of his writings, such as *The American Jitters* (1932), *To the Finland Station* (1940), *The Scrolls from the Dead Sea* (1955), *Apologies to the Iroquois* (1959), and *O Canada* (1965) range far beyond the province of literature. Wilson also wrote fiction, plays, and verse, recorded impressions of his travels to Soviet Russia, Israel, Haiti, and the main countries of Europe, and in several autobiographical writings left a full record of his development and views on all possible subjects. The diaries and notebooks that Leon Edel is editing and the collection of letters promised will constitute an account of a man's most initimate feelings and a chronicle of his involvement in his time from his first trip to Europe in 1908 to his last illness in 1972.

Thus some injustice is done if I limit myself strictly to the literary criticism. Focusing on it we are immediately confronted with two difficulties. Wilson himself disclaimed being a literary critic. "I think of myself simply as a writer and a journalist. I am as much interested in history as I am in literature," he said in 1959.[1] Then, as a good empiricist, Wilson refuses to be pinned down to a theory. In introducing his anthology, *The Shock of Recognition* (1943), Wilson states expressly that "the best way to understand the general is, in any case, to study the concrete."[2] There are only two essays in the enormous corpus of Wilson's writings that can be considered deliberate pronouncements on the theory of criticism and literature: "Marxism and Literature" (1937) and "The Historical Interpretation of Literature" (1941).[3] One must look to casual remarks and the implications of opinions and observations in order to discover the theories and standards that underlie his critical activity. One must be aware of the changes or at least the shifts of emphasis in his critical preoccupations, which run parallel to his political commitments, changing in turn with the social history of the United States.

It might be best first to define Wilson's position in a history of American criticism. Clearly he precedes the New Criticism, even though his career overlaps its heyday. Wilson never discusses any New Critic in detail. We find only perfunctory allusions, say, to Allen Tate's "finding fault with Keats for giving in to the emancipatory views of his time,"[4] or to Ransom's question about Shakespeare's reference to "dusty death,"[5] where even the name of Ransom is omitted, or to Empson's "interesting study of the Alice books."[6] Only in 1962 did Wilson comment on Leavis. He professes not to have read his books, "and when I have read him, he was always railing against somebody. He is the kind of dogmatic person who inevitably antagonizes me." "Why try to cast an anathema on somebody who doesn't like George Eliot? I detested *Silas Marner* and *Adam Bede* when I had to read them for school, and I've never got around to *Middlemarch*. And why regard Max Beerbohm as trivial?" Still, Wilson recognizes that Leavis's "interest in literature is passionate and moral."[7]

In the interview in which he speaks of the Leavis-Snow controversy about the two cultures without committing himself on the issue, Wilson tells of a plan to write "a sort of farce-melodrama of academic life." "The villain is a New Critic, who methodically takes Yeats's poems apart and discovers homosexuality in the 'Wild Swans at Coole'—note the 'Wilde' swans, and of course the swans are really young men."[8] Without mentioning names Wilson voices elsewhere his disapproval of "finding religious symbols and allegories in even such extremely nonreligious writers as Henry James and Stephen Crane," and he must be alluding to Leslie Fiedler's *Love and Death in the American Novel* (1960) when he complains about the assumption that "the sexual situations described in American fiction could only have taken place in America."[9] A similar passage refers to the "vast academic desert of the structure of *The Sound and the Fury,* the variants in the texts of *The Scarlet Letter* and the religious significance of *The Great Gatsby.*"[10] Wilson compares the present fashion of interpretation with the "technique of Jewish *pilpul,* that purely intellectual exercise which consists in explaining some passage from Scripture in a fantastically farfetched way."[11]

But these remarks seem off target. Neither strained psychoanalytical nor religious allegorizing is characteristic of the main New Critics, and they, of course, had no sympathy for the minute pedantries of textual criticism that Wilson attacked in his pamphlet, *The Fruits of the MLA* (1968). There seems a deliberate gingerly shrinking in Wilson's complete silence about I. A. Richards, Kenneth Burke, Yvor Winters, R. P. Blackmur, Cleanth Brooks, and F. O. Matthiessen, to mention only the most obvious names. He reviewed only Lionel Trilling's first book on *Matthew Arnold,* praising it but shirking a discussion of literary criticism.[12]

There is one exception, and that is T. S. Eliot, if we consider him a New Critic. Wilson early recognized that Eliot "has now [in 1929] become perhaps the most important literary critic in the English-speaking world"[13] and showed some surprise at the extent of Eliot's influence. "It is as much as one's life is worth nowadays, among young people, to say an approving word for Shelley or a dubious one about Donne." Wilson speaks, I think mistakenly, of Eliot's "scientific study of aesthetic values"[14] and recognizes that Eliot's criticism is "completely nonhistorical. He seemed to behold the writing of the age abstracted from time and space and spread before him in one great exhibition, of which, with imperturbable poise, he conducted a comparative appraisal."[15] In *Axel's Castle* Wilson wrote a whole page parodying Eliot's critical method: ridiculing his name-dropping and what to Wilson seemed irrelevant linkages and comparisons.[16] Wilson felt that the anti-Romantic reaction induced by Eliot is "leading finally into pedantry and into a futile aestheticism."[17]

Much later (in 1958) in a review of *The Sweeniad,* a satire on Eliot by "Myra Buttle," the pseudonym of Victor Purcell, a Cambridge classical don, Wilson defended Eliot. "It is silly to be outraged by his criticism of Shakespeare, Milton and Shelley." He agrees with Eliot that Dante's *Divine Comedy* "transcends any of Shakespeare's plays," that Milton's imagination is auditory rather than visual, and that Shelley writes loosely,[18] but he dislikes Eliot's impersonations of the "formidable professor," or of a revived Dr. Johnson who tries to instruct us "which poets of the past, and to what extent, it is permitted [us] to read and admire." He is irritated by Eliot's talk about the "Main Stream" of poetry, which seems to exclude Auden and even Yeats.[19] The dislike of Eliot's airs of a literary dictator is of course part and parcel of Wilson's disapproval of Eliot's politics and religion.

Wilson's distaste for the American New Humanists, Irving Babbitt and Paul Elmer More, is even stronger. The Humanists excited much public attention around 1929, but their doctrines were formulated much earlier, even in the 1890s and the first decade of this century. Wilson, in "Notes on Babbitt and More" (1930) and in an article "Sophocles, Babbitt and Freud" (1930), comments sharply disagreeing with Babbitt's interpretation of *Antigone.* Wilson had adopted a view of Greek tragedy that rejects the usual view of Sophocles' serenity, emphasizing rather the horror and violence of his plots, and objects particularly to the attempts, going back to Goethe, to play down Antigone's abnormal devotion to her brother.[20] Wilson in his polemics against Babbitt and More defends even "art for art's sake" as justified in its time, and argues for freedom of experimentation with such new techniques as the "stream of consciousness" in Joyce against More's uninformed sneers. More, he concludes, is "really an old-fashioned Puritan who has lost the Puritan theology without having lost the Puritan dogmatism,"[21] and Babbitt is called "an old-fashioned snob and pedant," "a fanatical literary moralist" who propounds an "aesthetically stupid philosophy."[22] Wilson had called on More at Princeton in December 1929 before his public attack and had written a somewhat satirical account of his visit that he published in a toned-down version, only after More's death in 1937.[23]

Thus Wilson is clearly set off from the two main trends of American criticism in the first half of this century. He has rather affinities with the group of critics who, around 1920, revolted against the "genteel tradition": with H. L. Mencken and Van Wyck Brooks. Wilson tells us how in 1912, at the age of seventeen, he came across *The Smart Set,* and was "astonished to find audacious and extremely amusing critical articles by men named Mencken and Nathan, of whom I had never heard."[24] Mencken is later praised in extravagant terms: "he is the civilized consciousness of modern America, its learning, its intelligence and its taste, realizing the grossness of its manners and mind and crying out in horror and chagrin."[25] With him "the whole perspective of literature in the United States was changed."[26] Wilson, however, came to recognize Mencken's unpleasant features: his contempt for the common man, "the great American boob," his pseudo-Nietzschean worship of the superman, and later his "tenderness to Nazis." Wilson admits that he can be "brutal, obtuse," that as a thinker he is "brash, inconsistent and crude," but he continued to admire him as "our greatest practicing journalist" since Poe, defending his "using a bludgeon on a society that understands nothing but bludgeons." Wilson particularly valued *The American Language* and praised his prose-style for its "personal rhythm and color." He was "a poet in prose and a humorist."[27]

In an invented dialogue between Scott Fitzgerald and Van Wyck Brooks, Wilson has Fitzgerald address Brooks: "You were almost alone, when you first began to write, in taking American literature seriously . . . you were among the first to stand for the romantic doctrine of experience for its own sake and to insist on the importance of literature as a political and social influence." Brooks understood that the failing of our literature was "the timidity of the 'genteel tradition.' "[28] "America's new orientation in respect to her artistic life was inaugurated in 1915 by Brooks's *America Coming of Age* and two years later more violently promoted by Mencken's *A Book of Prefaces.*"[29] When Brooks turned later into a sentimental, indiscriminate chronicler of American literary history with the series of books beginning with *The Flowering of New England* (1936), Wilson continued with his almost unstinting praise of Brooks though he himself had a far more critical view of the past of American literature. As late as 1963 Wilson called Brooks "one of the top American writers of our time," "the first modern literary historian to read through the whole of American belles lettres," comparing him, I think extravagantly, to the greatest literary historians, Francesco De Sanctis and Hippolyte Taine.[30]

Wilson reviewed every one of Brooks's books favorably, though he came to see that Brooks is not "really a literary critic because he is not interested in literature as an art and lies under serious suspicion of not being able to tell chalk from cheese ... Van Wyck Brooks concerns himself with literature mainly from the point of view of its immediate social significance." Still, he has "the historical imagination." He can "show us movements and books as they loomed upon the people to whom they were new."[31] Even the *Opinions of Oliver Allston* (1941), a deplorable book that divides writers into "primary," optimistic writers and the lesser breed of pessimists, is handled very gently by Wilson. It "revealed that [Brooks's] own standards of excellence are still more or less those of an enthusiastic young man in his twenties in the heyday of H. G. Wells, a young man for whom Tolstoy and Ibsen, on the one hand, and Victor Hugo and Browning, on the other, all inhabit the same empyrean of greatness."[32]

Wilson sees the change in Brooks from the "somber and despairing" early writings to the "chortling and crooning" *Flowering of New England*[33] and its successors, but he cannot bring himself to acknowledge Brooks's sellout to a bumptious nationalism, to the "nativism" that has since inflated the study of American literature.

Wilson sided with these critics of American business civilization in the twenties, but he differed from them as a critic in two crucial respects: he had a sure, well-defined taste, and he acquired tools for the analysis of literature from nineteenth-century historicism (particularly Marxism) and from Freud. He learned (if such a thing can be learned) his sense of quality very early in his school, Hill School in Pottstown, Pennsylvania. He speaks gratefully of his classical training, particularly of one teacher, Alfred Rolfe,[34] and of his early acquaintance with the writings of James Huneker, whose *Egoists* (1909) gave "a stimulating account of the excitement to be derived from the writings of Stendhal, Flaubert, Huysmans and Baudelaire."[35]

As an undergraduate at Princeton, class of 1916, Wilson studied French literature under Christian Gauss (1878–1951), with whom he established a lifelong, almost filial relationship. Gauss was, in Wilson's estimation (which lacks, I think, public documentation), "a brilliant critic—by far the best, as far as I know, in our academic world of that period."[36] In the dedication to Wilson's first critical book, *Axel's Castle* (1931), Wilson says that "it was principally from you that I acquired then my idea of what literary criticism ought to be—a history of man's ideas and imaginings in the setting of the conditions which have shaped them." The published correspondence shows how Wilson deferred to Gauss's advice[37] and how his taste was formed by an early immersion in French literature.

Wilson spent almost two years in France (from November 1917 to July 1919), first as a wound-dresser and then in intelligence. The war shook his aestheticism and what might be called his upperclass consciousness. (His father was a lawyer who had been New Jersey's attorney general for a brief period.) He realized that "I could never go back to the falseness and dullness of my prewar life again. I swore to myself that when the War was over I should stand outside society altogether."[38] After the Armistice he sent to friends a manifesto "indicting the institutions of the Western world and suggesting a way out in the direction of socialism."[39]

When he returned he plunged into the life of Greenwich Village and into journalism, first as managing editor of *Vanity Fair* and later as drama critic and associate editor of *The New Republic.* He became a declared dissenter, a "radical," a Bohemian, opposed to the reigning business temper of the time. He thus welcomed the stock market crash of 1929 with some glee as an exposure of the "stupid gigantic fraud" of capitalism.[40]

In the worst winter of the Depression (1930–31) Wilson went on extensive trips through the country investigating poverty, strikes, and racism such as the Scottboro case vividly described in *The American Jitters* (1932). Early in 1931 he studied Marx seriously for the first time, and he moved more and more toward communism, signing, for instance, a manifesto calling for the election of William Z. Foster for president in 1932. In 1935 Wilson made a trip to Russia for several months and wrote an account that, while showing some signs of disillusion, still asserted that "you feel in the Soviet Union that you are living at the moral top of the world."[41]

But Wilson very soon got into conflict with the orthodox communists, for he could not help being shocked by the great purges. Still, in 1940, he published *To the Finland Station*, a glowing account of the rise of socialism and communism, of the lives and teachings of Marx, Engels, Trotsky, and Lenin. Lenin is particularly admired as the propounder of "one of the great imaginative influences of our age—a world-view which gives life a meaning and in which every man is assigned a place." But Stalin is now called "a bandit-politician."[42]

That year Wilson broke with *The New Republic*: he opposed the pro-Allied policy of its owners. Wilson retired from public life almost completely, considering the war simply a struggle between two greedy imperialisms. In the summer of 1945 he made a trip to Europe as a reporter, a trip he then described in *Europe without Baedecker: Sketches among the Ruins of Italy, Greece and England* (1947). The book is a strange display of Wilson's American nationalism and feeling of superiority over the little nations of Europe (England and France included).

Despite all the criticism of American policies, Wilson had remained a strong nationalist. As early as 1928 Wilson said that it "is our high destiny to step in and speak the true prophetic words to declining Europe."[43] Even in 1956 Wilson could assert that "for myself, as an American, I have not the least doubt that I have derived a good deal more benefit of the civilizing as well as the inspirational kind from the admirable American bathroom than I have from the cathedrals of Europe," though in the same book of reflections, *A Piece of My Mind*, he could also declare: "When, for example, I look through *Life* magazine, I feel that I do not belong to the country depicted there, that I do not even live in that country."[44]

Wilson did not file income tax returns from 1946 to 1955, and he defended this lapse in a pamphlet entitled *The Cold War and the Income Tax* (1936) with a violent attack on American bureaucracy and policies. He accepted all the cliches of the opposition: Roosevelt lured the United States into the war, the Cold War was started by the Americans, it was merely a struggle between two greedy seaslugs or gorillas.

Just at the time when he felt most strongly opposed to American policies and had almost stopped commenting on contemporary American literature, he was widely honored. In 1963 he received the Presidential Medal of Freedom, and later the

National Medal for Literature. He enjoyed the rewards of the Establishment with the privilege of rebelling against it. In academic circles his reputation had been low since Stanley Hyman's unfair chapter in *The Armed Vision* (1948), but it rose again in the last years of his life when Sherman Paul, Charles P. Frank, and Leonard Kriegel published sympathetic monographs and Frank Kermode, John Wain, Alfred Kazin, Norman Podhoretz, and others wrote laudatory articles.[45]

It seemed necessary to trace Wilson's political opinions because his criticism reflects these changes very accurately. Long before the dedication to Gauss, Wilson must have been aware of the historical setting and even conditioning of literature. He tells us that at the age of fifteen he had read Hippolyte Taine's *History of English Literature* in translation and that his "whole point of view about literature was affected by Taine's methods of presentation and interpretation." Later he read Taine in French and admired particularly the comparison between Tennyson and Musset.[46] Wilson's admiration for this passage, which confronts the audience of Tennyson—the family circle, the world travelers, the connoisseurs of antiquity, the sportsmen, the lovers of the countryside, the wealthy Victorian businessmen and their ladies—with that of Musset—the intellectuals, the Bohemian artists, the earnest specialists, the hectic women of leisure—survived the cooling-off that we feel in the chapter on Taine in *To the Finland Station,* in which Wilson disagrees with Taine's hostile view of the French revolution. Wilson deplores here the "monotonous force" of his style, the "cocksure and priggish tone." Taine "manages to combine the rigor of the factory with the upholstery and the ornamentation of the nineteenth-century *salon,*" but Wilson still admires Taine's scientific program, which he sees modified by "strong moral prepossessions."

From Taine and, I assume, from many other historians Wilson drew general concepts of determinism, or at least genetic causation.[47] He frequently refers to the racial ancestry of authors; in the case of Oscar Wilde we must take into account his Italian blood "in considering his theatrical instincts and his appetite for the ornate."[48] Wilson makes much of the moral genius of the Jews. "It was probably the Jew in the half-Jewish Proust that saved him from being the Anatole France of an even more deliquescent phase of the French belletristic tradition."[49] He even appeals to the elusive inheritance of a grandfather's char-

71

acter when he explains Ronald Firbank's passion for perfection by the slogan of his grandfather, a big railroad contractor: "I value as nowt what I gets for nowts."[50]

As in Taine, great importance is sometimes assigned to climate and weather: we are told that Genevieve Taggard was born in the state of Washington and taken as a baby to Honolulu, and we are asked "whether the moods and the emotions of lyric poetry are not, to a considerable degree, the products of varying weather. In countries where the seasons change, our feelings also run to extremes." In California even poetry becomes equable and bright as the climate.[51]

Wilson seems to believe in a linguistic determinism when he says that "our failure in the United States to produce much first-rate lyric poetry is partly due to our flattening and drawling of the vowels and our slovenly slurring of the consonants,"[52] and he makes much of the Russian aspects of verbs to conclude that Russians lack a sense of time—and this explains the length of their novels and plays.[53] He can even establish a link between the progress of technology and a literary genre. For instance, the ghost story was killed by electric light. "It was only during the ages of candlelight that the ghost story really flourished."[54] Once he makes the odd statement that value is determined by demand: "If Manet cannot possibly be considered so great a painter as Titian, it is partly because, in his lifetime, there was so much less demand for his work."[55]

More convincingly, throughout his career Wilson would point to the social origins of a writer such as Ben Jonson or Max Beerbohm.[56] He would try to reconstruct the background, for example, in the politics of Upstate New York during the Civil War in order to explain the stories of Harold Frederic[57] or treat the novels of Harriet Beecher Stowe as " 'a great repository' that contains solid chunks of history,"[58] drawing from literature a social picture of the time.

More boldly he would generalize on the spirit of all age or time. Thus Dorothy Parker's poetry belongs to the "general tone, the psychological and literary atmosphere of the period," to the Twenties, "when people were much freer" than in the Thirties, when "they began to have to watch their pockets" and their politics. He looks back at the Twenties, when "the idea of the death of a society had not yet begun working on people to paralyze their response to experience."[59] Wilson's first book of criticism, *Axel's Castle* (1931), implies such generalizations about succeeding time-spirits. Wilson himself acknowledges that the scheme of Alfred North Whitehead's *Science and the Modern World* (1926) suggested the plan of his book.[60]

Just as Romanticism (as interpreted in Whitehead's book) reacted against the Newtonian science of the eighteenth century, so Symbolism reacted against the Naturalism, Darwinism, and Positivism of the nineteenth century. As early as 1926 Wilson conceived the idea of an international symbolist movement which, I believe, was new at that time.[61] The grouping of Yeats, Valéry, Eliot, Proust, Joyce, and Gertrude Stein was an insight developed only much later. It was 1933 before Valéry Larbaud proclaimed Proust a symbolist.[62]

This concept of the unity and continuity of the international movement and the selection of the great names was Wilson's. We may, however, have doubts about the inclusion of Gertrude Stein and note Wilson's blind spot: his ignoring of the Germans—George, Rilke, and Thomas Mann. We may doubt Wilson's success in attempting to stress the concepts of space-time and relativity implied in Proust and Joyce as being the equivalent of the metaphysics of Whitehead. "As in the universe of Whitehead, the 'events,' which may be taken arbitrarily as infinitely small or infinitely comprehensive, make up an organic structure, in which all are interdependent, each involving every other and the whole; so Proust's book is a gigantic dense mesh of complicated revelations." Joyce is assimilated to Proust in these terms: "Like Proust's or Whitehead's or Einstein's world, Joyce's world is always changing as it is perceived by different observers and by them at different times."[63]

But the claim that these symbolists (in Wilson's sense) reflect or incorporate the most advanced insights of modern physical science and even point to an ultimate union of art and science can hardly be sustained. Oddly enough, instead of endorsing Valéry's similar hope, Wilson disparages Valéry as a philosopher. "Most of Valéry's reputation for profundity comes, I believe, from the fact that he was one of the first literary men to acquire a smattering of the new mathematical and physical theory." "He never seems to have gotten over his excitement at reading Poincaré."[64]

This whole concept is in conflict with the side of symbolism that Wilson cannot help stressing: "a sullenness, a lethargy, a

sense of energies ingrown and sometimes festering." Wilson calls
A la recherche du temps perdu "one of the gloomiest books ever
written," evokes the aridity and dreariness of Eliot's *The Waste
Land*, and even says of Yeats that his poetry is "dully weighted,
for all its purity and candor, by a leaden acquiescence in de-
feat." Joyce, however, is exempted. "It is curious to reflect that
a number of critics . . . should have found Joyce misanthropic."[65]

Axel's Castle is, however, dominated by other motifs: Wilson's
view that verse is a dying technique, that verse is a thing of the
past, and that symbolism will be or should be replaced by a
new naturalism. There seems to be a shift in Wilson's view during the writing of the book. The first chapter on "Symbolism,"
originally published as "A Preface to Modern Literature" in
March 1929, gives a sympathetic account of the French symbolist movement, whereas the last chapter, "Axel and Rimbaud," originally published in February and March 1930 after
the stock market crash, has a tone of disapproval.[66] We are told
that "the only originality of the Symbolists consisted in reminding people of the true nature and function of words,"[67] i.e., their
power of suggestion. We are then treated to a contrast between
the fictional Axel (in Villiers de l'Isle-Adam's tragedy) who says,
"Live? our servants will do that for us," and the life story of
Rimbaud, told with the embellishments then current, concluding that "Rimbaud's life seems more satisfactory than the
works of his Symbolist contemporaries."[68] He hopes now that we
shall live to see Valéry, Eliot, and Yeats displaced, and he
points suddenly to Russia as "a country where a central socio-
political idealism has been able to use and to inspire the artist
as well as the engineer."[69] Wilson has been converted to Marxism.

But has he become a Marxist literary critic? The question
cannot be answered by a simple "yes" or "no." Wilson certainly
becomes conscious of the class concept and the economic conditions of literature. When Michael Gold, a Marxist critic, attacked Thornton Wilder as a typical bourgeois, Wilson, though
a friend of Wilder, defended Gold for raising the class issue.[70]
Occasionally Wilson engaged in Marxist allegorizing. Thus, referring to the fact that we are told at the end of the novel that
Madame Bovary's daughter is sent to a cotton mill after her
mother's suicide, Wilson remarks: "The socialist of Flaubert's

74

time might perfectly have approved of this: while the romantic individualist deludes himself with unrealizable fantasies, in the attempt to evade bourgeois society, and only succeeds in destroying himself, he lets humanity fall a victim to the industrial-commercial processes, which, unimpeded by his dreaming, go on with their deadly work."[71] But even here Wilson does not quite endorse this interpretation put into the mouth of a socialist of Flaubert's time: Wilson must have been aware that the fate of poor Berthe is quite incidental to the meaning of the book. At most, it adds one more cruel touch. In the same paper, "The Politics of Flaubert" (1937), the liaison between Rosanette, the daughter of poor silk-mill workers, with the hero of *L'éducation sentimentale*, Frédéric Moreau, is considered "a symbol of the disastrously unenduring union between the proletariat and the bourgeoisie, of which Karl Marx had written in *The Eighteenth Brumaire*."[72] But this paper is an exception.

In 1938 Wilson discussed "Marxism and Literature," expressly quoting some of the standard texts: Engels's 1890 letter to Starkenburg, admitting a reciprocal interaction between the economic base and the superstructure; the letter of Engles to Minna Kautsky, disapproving of overtly tendentious novels; the Sickingen debate with Lassalle, which Wilson reduces to Marx chiding Lassalle for mistaking the role of his hero; and the passage that praises Greek art and grants that "certain periods of highest development of art stand in no direct connection with the general development of society, nor with the material basis and the skeleton structure of its organization."[73] Wilson sees this passage only as an inconsistency without discussing the issue itself, and he continues briefly to expound Lenin's essays on Tolstoy, accepting their thesis that Tolstoy represents the psychology of patriarchal peasantry.

Wilson is most impressed by Trotsky's *Literature and Revolution* (1924), agreeing with him that there cannot be a proletarian literature and that a work of art must first be judged as a work of art. Wilson sees that the identification of literature with politics is liable to terrible abuses, and he deplores developments under Stalin such as the damning of the music of Shostakovich. He concludes that "Marxism by itself can tell us nothing whatever about the goodness or badness of a work of art": a conclusion that rejects, in principle, all the efforts of Marxists such as Lukács to develop a specific Marxist aesthetics. "What Marxism can do, however, is throw a great deal of light on the origins and social significance of works of art."[74]

Wilson seems to allude to a view like that of Lukács (though I know of no evidence that he had read or could have read him at that time) when he denies that "the character of a work of art" must be "shown engaged in a conflict which illustrates the larger conflicts of society." What matters is the moral insight. Wilson gives the death of Bergotte in Proust's novel and, rather incongruously, Thornton Wilder's *Heaven's My Destination* and Hemingway's story, "The Undefeated," as examples of apparently trivial subjects widening into universal significance. Narrowly prescriptive requirements such as Granville Hicks's requirement that the author's point of view must be "that of the vanguard of the proletariat" are rejected, as is the doctrine of "socialist realism" as a futile attempt "to legislate masterpieces into existence."[75]

Wilson distinguishes between "short-range and long-range" literature (like Ruskin's "books for the moment" versus "books for the ages"), recognizing that art can be and has been a political weapon. But what remains of Dante is not his commitment to the Emperor Henry or the commitment of Shakespeare to "Elizabethan imperialism." In general, Wilson argues, revolutionary periods were not periods of great creative upsurge in literature. Wilson can think only of Chénier and Blok, and they hardly prove the opposite: Chénier was guillotined and Blok died in despair with the revolution in Russia.

But at the end of the article Wilson embraces the most Utopian side of Marxist doctrine. "It is society itself, says Trotsky, which under communism becomes the work of art." Wilson knows that "this is to speak in terms of centuries, of ages; but, in practicing and prizing literature, we must not be unaware of the first efforts of the human spirit to transcend literature itself."[76] The odd ideal of a humanity that can and should dispense with art—apparently beginning to be realized in Soviet Russia—is evoked somewhat hesitantly. I believe that this passage, though anticipated in the recently published notebooks,[77] is unique in Wilson's public writings.

The Princeton lecture on "The Historical Interpretation of Literature" (1940), which followed the papers on Marxism three years later, rehearses the same topics under a different title and in a markedly subdued tone. Wilson glances at the origins of

76

the historical approach in Vico (a figure briefly discussed also in connection with his discoverer, Michelet, in *To the Finland Station*), Herder, Hegel, and Taine. Taine and Michelet, Wilson observes, paid attention to the influence of social classes before Marx. Marx and Engels as literary critics were "tentative, confused and modest."

Again the passage on Greek art is singled out as giving Marx "a good deal of trouble." Bernard Shaw and Franz Mehring are mentioned as "the great critics who were trained on Marx," and Trotsky's *Literature and Revolution* is called "brilliant and valuable."[78] But now a new motif is introduced: Psychoanalysis, or simply "the interpretation of works of literature in the light of personalities behind them." Wilson thinks of Freudian psychoanalysis merely as an extension of the biographical interpretation as practiced by Dr. Johnson and Sainte-Beauve. He praises Van Wyck Brooks's *The Ordeal of Mark Twain* (1920) as a model. "The attitudes, the compulsions, the emotional 'patterns' that recur in the work of a writer are of great interest to the historical critic." Freudian, individual psychology is assimilated to the historical method which, in turn, has absorbed the Marxist approach. Wilson advocates such a combination, but he sees that the historical (or, better, simply the genetic) approach does not solve the problem of criticism as value judgment. He repeats the argument stated in the Marxism paper. "No matter how thoroughly and searchingly we may have scrutinized works of literature from the historical and biographical point of view, we must be ready to attempt to estimate ... the relative degrees of success attained by the products of the various periods and the various personalities. We must be able to tell good from bad, the first-rate from the second-rate. We shall not otherwise write literary criticism at all, but merely social or political history as reflected in literary texts, or psychological case histories from past eras."[79]

Wilson solves the question of value judgment to his satisfaction by an appeal to an emotional reaction that he considers the Kantian solution as he learned it from his Princeton teacher, Norman Kemp Smith. Attempts to define standards such as "unity, symmetry, originality, vision, inspiration, strangeness, suggestiveness, improving morality, socialist realism," do not impress him: "you simply shift the emotional reaction to the recognition of the element or elements" and still might not have a good play, a good novel, a good poem. This reliance on taste leads Wilson to accept a self-appointed and self-perpetuating elite of "genuine connoisseurs who establish standards of taste" and "will compel you to accept their authority." Wilson trusts, far too easily, that "imposters may try to put themselves over, but these quacks will not last."[80] He believes in the verdict of the ages.

The appeal to taste is nothing new. For instance, in 1927 he is content to say: "I do not pretend that my own primary judgments as to what is good poetry or what is not are anything other, in the last analysis, than mysterious emotional responses,"[81] and he even seems to endorse the silly criterion for poetry proposed by A. E. Housman, tongue-in-cheek, that "the most intense, the most profound, the most beautifully composed and the most comprehensive works of literary art . . . are also the most thrilling and give us most prickly sensations while shaving."[82]

Wilson preserved an admiration for the "gusto" of Saintsbury, the intensity of the poetic effect propounded by Poe. Saintsbury is called the "sole full-length professional critic, who is of really first-rate stature," "a gourmet and something of a glutton" for whom "the enjoyment of literature [is] somehow a moral matter."[83] Wilson here seems to define his own attitude and prevalent practice: conveying the joy of literature by describing, evoking, or often simply summarizing the books he has read. As he said himself: "There are few things I enjoy so much as talking to people about books which I have read and they haven't, and making them wish they had—particularly a book that is hard to get or in a language that they do not know."[84]

Many times Wilson deplores the decline of "appreciation" in favor of purely technical or philosophical or sociological treatment of literature.[85] The bulk of his criticism is undeniably that of an "introductory critic," a middleman, an expositor and chronicler of literary events, a role that we should not underrate in its effects on several generations of readers nor underrate for the sheer abilities it requires in the skill, say, of retelling Proust's series of novels or the numerous memoirs of the Civil War in *Patriotic Gore*. But, of course, Wilson's ideal of the critic goes beyond this function. A reviewer-critic should know "the past work of every important writer he deals with and be able to write about an author's new book in the light of his general development and intention. He should also be able to see the author in relation to the national literature and the national literature in relation to other literatures."[86] In "A Modest Self-tribute" (1952) Wilson quite rightly claims to have "tried to contribute a little to the general cross-fertilization, to make it possible for our literate public to appreciate and to understand both our Anglo-American culture and those of the European countries in relation to one another."[87]

Though Wilson detested the American Humanists, he arrives at a humanism of his own: "the belief in the nobility and beauty of what man as man has accomplished, and the reverence for literature as a record of this." Since his school years, "humanism had continued to serve me when the religion had come to seem false. The thing that glowed for me through Xenophon and Homer in those classrooms of thirty years ago has glowed for me ever since."[88]

Marxism remains firmly relegated to being a variety of the historical approach. As the discussion of Marx in *To the Finland Station* shows, Wilson, though deeply impressed by Marx's personality, devotion, and moral fervor in criticizing the industrial society of his time, came away from a study of his writings totally unconvinced by two crucial Marxist doctrines: the surplus value and the dialectic. Marx's Labor theory is rejected as "the creation of the metaphysician," fallacious because of its narrow concept of human motivation, and the dialectic is dismissed as a "religious myth disencumbered of a divine personality and tied up with the history of mankind." Dialectic is simply the "old Trinity": "the mythical and magical triangle . . . which probably derived its significance from its correspondence to the male sexual organs," a hoary joke of anti-Trinitarian polemics.[89]

History in Marxism is "a substitute for old-fashioned Providence."[90] Wilson consistently criticized overt propaganda art. "There is no sense," he says in discussing "Communist Criticism" (1937), "in pursuing a literary career under the impression that one is operating a bombing plane."[91] Marxist criticism does not recognize that "there are groups which cut through the social classes, and these tend to have an independent existence. The writers make a group of their own; the painters make a group of their own; the scientists make a group. And each of these groups has its own tradition, its own craft and body of doctrine which has been brought down to the present by practitioners that have come from a variety of classes through a variety of societies. . . . A Communist critic who, in reviewing a book, ignores the author's status as a craftsman is really, for purposes of propaganda, denying the dignity of human work."[92] In quite a different context Wilson illustrates this idea, admitting that Virgil was not possible without Augustus—but also without Apollonius Rhodius, his Alexandrian predecessor, the poet of the *Argonautica*.[93]

Wilson had learned from Marxism that "economic and social forces do play a much larger part in molding people's ideals, and consequently in coloring their literature, than most people are willing to admit,"[94] but he did not adopt either the concept of history or the commitment to the cause of literature furthering the aims of Marxism. Proletarian literature does not and cannot exist, just as "there could not be proletarian chemistry or proletarian engineering." "When the proletariat learn to appreciate the arts . . . they will appreciate and understand them in the same way as anyone else." "There are already great proletarian artists and scientists, not of proletarians."[95] The involvement of art in ideology and class is denied: a universal art and even universal human nature is assumed here. Marxism is rejected.

In contrast, Wilson's interest in psychoanalysis grew, and the book *The Wound and the Bow* (1941) is expressly devoted to the problem. Wilson had known about psychoanalysis before. One of his earliest papers, "The Progress of Psychoanalysis," dates back to 1920.[96] Wilson's interest in an author's psychology was not merely biographical. He assumes, in the discussion of Proust, that "the real elements, of course, of any work of fiction, are the elements of the author's personality: his imagination embodies in the images of characters, situations and scenes the fundamental conflicts of his nature or the cycles of phases through which it habitually passes. His personages are personifications of the author's various impulses and emotions."[97]

But only in *The Wound and the Bow* is the connection between psychic disease and artistic accomplishment stated as a thesis. The title essay, the last in the book, uses the Philoctetes story from Sophocles' play. "The victim of a maladorous disease . . . is also the master of a superhuman art."[98] But one could object that the Philoctetes story does not lend itself as a model for the "conception of superior strength as inseparable from disability"

or the idea "that genius and disease, like strength and mutila-
tion, may be inextricably bound together,"[99] as Wilson seems to
claim. Philoctetes had the miraculous bow before he was bitten
by the snake. The story does not imply that the bow may not
be owned or drawn without the wound.

But we must not press the parallel; we should be content
with the Philoctetes story simply as an allegory of the situations
described in several essays of the book. "Dickens: The Two
Scrooges" emphasizes the shock of the six months the twelve-
year-old boy spent laboring in a blacking warehouse; "The
Kipling Nobody Read" exploits the degrading experiences of
Kipling as a little boy with foster parents in England slightly
fictionalized in the story "Baa Baa Black Sheep," and his further brutalizing at the United Services College, oddly glorified
in *Stalky and Co.* The other essays in the volume hardly fit the
formula of the title. But even the pieces on Dickens and Kipling
cannot be reduced to mere exemplifications of the theory. They
are also essays using the traditional methods of criticism. In the
Dickens essay Wilson is looking for the darker side of Dickens at
the expense of his humor. Dickens's interest in criminals and
rebels, in thieves and murderers, in scenes of violence such as
hangings or the burning of Newgate prison in *Barnaby Rudge,*
and in his general revolt against the institutions and the temper
of the age and its representative, the Queen, whom he studi-
ously avoided meeting, is skillfully expounded. In his last unfin-
ished novel, *The Mystery of Edwin Drood,* "Dickens has turned,"
Wilson claims, "the protest against the age into a protest against
self." Wilson sees Dickens accepting the verdict that "he is a
creature irretrievably tainted,"[100] a conclusion that seems war-
ranted only if we assume that the murderer Jasper somehow
embodies the submerged mind of Dickens himself.[101] But the essay was deservedly influential in changing the accepted image of
the jolly Christmas Dickens, though Wilson's own picture seems
overdrawn in the other direction.

Similarly, the essay on Kipling, though it makes much of the
boy's tribulations by explaining how "the work of [his] life is to
be shot through with hatred," soon becomes straight literary
criticism. *Stalky and Co.* is the worst of Kipling's books, "crude in
writing, trashy in feeling," whereas *Kim* is almost a first-rate
book.[102] But psychological criteria are used on occasion. The
concept of overcompensation seems to be invoked when we are

told that it is "proof of Kipling's timidity and weakness that he should loudly overdo this glorification" of his motherland. It seems hard, however, to understand "the ferocious antagonism to democracy which finally overtakes him must have been fed by the fear of that household in Southsea which tried to choke his genius at its birth."[103] It assumes that the boy Kipling saw democracy embodied in the ferocious tyranny of his guardians and that he knew of his genius at that time. Even *The Light that Failed,* Wilson argues, shows that "the theme of anguish which is suffered without being deserved [i.e., the hero going blind] has the appearance of having been derived from a morbid permanent feeling of injury inflicted by his experience at Southsea." The whole attempt to derive every theme from these childhood experiences seems often forced: thus, "Mary Postgate," the story of a soldier killed in an airplane, is considered to illustrate the "theme of the abandoned parent" (actually a plain and dull companion who stood in a maternal role to the soldier) as "reflecting in reversal the theme of abandoned child."[104] As often in psychoanalysis, it is: "Heads or tails, you lose."

We must look beyond *The Wound and the Bow* for Wilson's use of psychoanalytical insights. "The Ambiguity of Henry James" in *The Triple Thinkers* is the best-known essay that interprets *The Turn of the Screw* as "a neurotic case of sex repression." "The ghosts are not real ghosts but hallucinations of the governess."[105] Wilson's view is easily refuted not only by Henry James's express declaration in the *Notebooks* (published after Wilson's essay), but by the obvious fact (which Wilson tries to dispute, however) that "Mrs. Gross, the housekeeper, recognizes the dead valet in the highly specific description of the sinister intruder given by the governess, who had never before heard of Peter Quint."[106] While the paper seems mistaken in its attempt to psychologize James's ghost story, it does perceptively discuss James's preoccupation with the "conception of a man shut out from love, condemned to peep at other people's activities," "dramatizing the frustrations of his own life."[107] In a postscript to the essay (1948) Wilson accepts the psychoanalytical interpretation by Dr. Saul Rosenzweig of James's accident during a fire at Newport, Rhode Island, in 1861 (when he was eighteen), but backs away from its full implication when he disowns the idea of "reducing the dignity of these stories by reading into them the embarrassments of the author."[108] Much of the paper is straight literary criticism. Thus Wilson singles out the first volume of *The Tragic Muse* as "solid and alive," as James's "best novel," and condemns *The Awkward Age* "for combining a lifeless trickery of logic with the equivocal subjectivity of a nightmare."[109] Wilson won a prize as a Princeton undergraduate with an essay on Henry James[110] and preserved for him a lifelong affection and not uncritical admiration. Unlike Van Wyck Brooks (and F. R. Leavis) Wilson cherishes the last novels of Henry James. "Intellectually, they are perhaps the most vigorous, the most heroically conceived, of his fictions."[111]

Wilson became technically psychoanalytical only when he used Freud's article "Charakter und Analerotik" (1908) or some of its derivatives to characterize Ben Jonson. He finds in Ben Jonson the three traits—pedantry, avarice, and obstinacy—ascribed by Freud to childhood attitudes toward excretory processes. Avarice appears in literature as a hoarding of words. Wilson, however, suddenly retreats from his commitment to the Freudian approach. "I am not qualified to 'analyze' Jonson in the light of this Freudian conception, and I have no interest in trying to fit him into any formulation of it. I am not even sure that the relation between the workings of the alimentary tract and the other phenomena of personality is, as Freud assumes, a relation of cause and effect; but I am sure that Freud has here really seized upon a nexus of human traits that are involved with one another and has isolated a recognizable type."[112] Thus "anal eroticism" in Wilson has come to mean nothing more than a psychological type, a pattern of character traits exhibited in the life and writings of Ben Jonson and apparently also in Gogol and Joyce.[113] But I cannot see that the recurrent themes of Ben Jonson's plays, "miserliness, unsociability, a self-sufficient and systematic spite," prove anything about Ben Jonson as a person or why a character like Morose (the man pathologically and comically afraid of noise in *The Silent Woman*) shows Ben Jonson "tormenting himself for what is negative and recessive in his nature."[114] Ben Jonson, to my mind, has fun at the expense of a miser and wants his audience to laugh at his plight and gloat over his falling into a trap. Wilson underestimates the role of genre, of stage stereotypes and theatrical conventions.

Wilson defends the interest in individual psychology as compatible with the historical method and with Marxism. "The attitudes, the compulsions, the emotional 'patterns' that recur in the work of a writer are of great interest to the historical critic. These attitudes and patterns are embodied in the community and the historical moment, and they may indicate its ideals and its diseases as the cell shows the condition of the tissue. The recent scientific experimentation [I am not sure what Wilson can be referring to] in the combining of Freudian with Marxist method, and of psychoanalysis with anthropology, has had its parallel development in criticism." While welcoming this combination Wilson always sees the limits of any genetic approach. "Freud himself emphatically states in his study of Leonardo that his method can make no attempt to account for Leonardo's genius. The problems of comparative artistic value still remain after we have given attention to the Freudian psychological factor just as they do after we have given attention to the Marxist economic factor and to the racial and geographical factors."[115]

Only rarely can we discover Wilson's criteria for artistic value. It is clear that poetry is judged by Wilson quite inadequately: he inherited, possibly from Saintsbury, a distinction between content and form that made form largely mean conventional versification and euphonious sound effects. Verse to him is "a technique," and a "dying technique" at that.[116] He rejects the narrowing of the concept of poetry to lyrical verse, protesting Valéry's view that poetry is "absolutely different in kind from prose," that it is "all suggestion, while prose is all sense."[117]

Historically, Wilson argues, verse was used for all kinds of purposes. In antiquity Lucretius and Virgil used it for philosophical argument or for instruction in agriculture; Victorians like the Brownings wrote novels in verse; in recent times the use of poetry is confined to the description or expression of emotion.[118] But Wilson draws from this specialization of the concept of poetry, which parallels the "purification" of the other arts, the unwarranted conclusion that verse is destined to disappear. This is justified by a theory that verse, being "a more primitive technique than prose," is losing its early association with music and has become "occular." One can understand that Wilson disliked the blank verse of Maxwell Anderson[119] and had his doubts about the success of modern verse drama as advocated by T. S. Eliot, but surely his forecast of the disappearance of verse is not likely to be fulfilled, considering the enormous output even in industrialized societies, not to speak of other countries and languages where verse has kept its dominance.

Wilson reviewed many poets and wrote poetry himself, much of it humorous and parodic, but his relation to it remains unsure, awkward, even hostile, and his vocabulary in dealing with it is often vague and imprecise. He quickly slides into a discussion of theme and ideology and makes many egregious blunders in his estimates.

Emily Dickinson seems to him "a little overrated,"[120] Robert Frost is "excessively dull and he certainly writes very poor verse."[121] E. E. Cummings is an "eternal adolescent," "as half-baked as a schoolboy," expressing "familiar and simple emotions," but at least he is not, like Wallace Stevens, "insulated or chilled; he is not indifferent to life." Stevens suffers "from a sort of aridity" but remains "a charming decorative artist."[122] Auden has "arrested at the mentality of an adolescent schoolboy," though later Wilson recognized him as "an incredible virtuoso."[123] Pound's poems are "a pile of fragments." "In spite of the parade of culture and the pontifical pretenses, Ezra Pound is really at heart a very boyish fellow and an incurable provincial."[124]

Some of these jibes, no doubt, have their measure of truth, but even in the sympathetic discussions Wilson's limitations as a critic of poetry are glaring. The chapter about Yeats in *Axel's Castle* manages to ignore such poems as "The Second Coming" (1921) or "Sailing to Byzantium" (1928). Wilson criticizes Yeats for what in recent jargon has been called "elitism," his "dignity and distinction" "becoming more and more impossible in our modern democratic society," for his aloofness from the "democratic, the scientific, the modern world," "from the general enlightened thought of his time." Wilson is comprehensibly impatient with *A Vision,* which he contrasts with the so much more sensible *Intelligent Woman's Guide to Socialism and Capitalism* by Bernard Shaw.[125]

The essay on T. S. Eliot in the same book excels in suggesting the personal sources of Eliot's views. *The Waste Land* illustrates "the peculiar conflicts of the Puritan turned artist, the horror of vulgarity and the shy sympathy with the common life, the ascetic shrinking from sexual experience and the distress at the drying up of the springs of sexual emotion, with the straining after a religious emotion which may be made to take its place."[126] A diary entry is even more perceptive in saying that *The Waste Land* is "nothing more nor less than a most dis-

85

tressingly moving account of Eliot's own agonized state of mind during the years which preceded his nervous breakdown." "It is certainly a cry *de profundis* if there ever was one—almost the cry of a man on the verge of insanity."[127] Wilson, however, never tried to say anything about the *Four Quartets*.

In poetic taste Wilson remains an incurable imagist who admires the music of smooth verse and the vividness of visual metaphors in Edna St. Vincent Millay, Elinor Wylie, or Genevieve Taggard, poets he greatly overrated, and not only for personal reasons. Music and image somehow combined or fused are his ideal of poetry.

He is much more satisfactory and much more concrete when he speaks of the novel. A great novelist "must show us large social forces, or uncontrollable lines of destiny, or antagonistic impulses of the human spirit, struggling with one another."[128] The idea, old enough, of the need of contraries in art is developed also as an argument against propaganda art. "One of the primary errors of recent radical criticism has been the assumption that great novels and plays must necessarily be written by people who have everything clear in their minds. People who have everything clear in their minds, who are not capable of identifying themselves imaginatively with, who do not actually embody in themselves, contrary emotions and points of view, do not write novels or plays at all—do not, at any rate, write good ones. And—given genius—the more violent the contraries, the greater the works of art."[129]

Somewhat surprisingly this criterion of violent contraries, apparently not necessarily reconciled, is used to put down *War and Peace* as not "quite one of the very summits of literature" because of its "idyllic tendency," for "a certain element of the idealization in which we are all disposed to indulge in imagining the lives of our ancestors."[130] One could argue that *War and Peace* shows violent contraries: war and peace, age and youth, good and evil, and so forth, more than most novels, but Wilson has a point in feeling the nostalgia that permeates many scenes. In all of these passages nothing suggests anything but a clash of contraries.

But when Wilson reads Pushkin's *Evgeny Onegin*, which he admires almost beyond any other work of literature, he feels as if he were watching the process "by which the several elements of [Pushkin's] character, the several strands of his experience, have

86

taken symmetry about the foci of distinct characters." Pushkin's "serenity, his perfect balance of tenderness for human beings with unrelenting respect for reality, show a rarer quality of mind than Stendhal's."[131]

Balance, equipoise is not quite resolution, reconciliation. But in a few passages Wilson thinks of art in these terms. "That was the paradox of literature: provoked by the anomalies of reason, by its discord, its chaos, its pain, it attempted, from poetry to metaphysics, to impose on that chaos some order, to find some resolution for that discord, to render the pain acceptable."[132] Sometimes Wilson conceives this ordering and consoling function of literature in crass utilitarian terms: "All our intellectual activity, in whatever field it takes place, is an attempt to give meaning to our experience—that is, to make life more practicable; for by understanding things we make it easier to survive and get around among them." Immediately afterwards the function of literature is again defined as curative: "We have been cured of some ache of disorder, relieved of some oppressive burden of uncomprehended events."[133] It sounds almost like Wordsworth speaking of the "lightening of the burden of the mystery."

In the upshot, Wilson seems to require some basic optimism from a writer. Thus he prefers Steinbeck to Aldous Huxley because of Steinbeck's "irreducible faith in life." Referring to *After Many a Summer Dies the Swan*, Wilson says: "we shall be more likely to find out something of value for the control and ennoblement of life by studying human behavior in this spirit than through the code of self-contemplation that seems to grow so rootlessly and palely in the decay of scientific tradition which this latest of the Huxleys represents."[134]

Similarly Wilson complains about the stories in Angus Wilson's *The Wrong Set*, saying that "we end by being repelled and by feeling that it is not quite decent to enjoy so much ugliness and humiliation. There ought to be some noble value somewhere."[135] On occasion Wilson seems, however, to consider this idealizing function of literature simply a fraud. He can say that "art has its origin in the need to pretend that human life is something other than it is, and, in a sense, by pretending this, it succeeds to some extent in transforming it."[136] But in a discussion of Dostoevsky we are told that "the work of art has only the dignity of any other self-protective movement." Dostoevsky

87

"has falsified life, because he has pretended to harmonize something." "The work of art is therefore an imposture."[137]

But this imposture, this beautiful lie, is ultimately seen as a noble necessity. Wilson wrote a crude and obtuse essay, "A Dissenting Opinion on Kafka" (1946), which argues that it is impossible "to take him seriously as a major writer," but the objections to his presumed pessimism and religious mysticism come from a deep core of Wilson's nature. When he quotes in conclusion Kafka's aphorism "one must not cheat anybody, not even the world of its triumph," Wilson protests. "But what are we writers here for if it is not to cheat the world of its triumph?"[138] This is why he was so impressed by André Malraux's *Voices of Silence*, "one of the really great books of our time": Malraux believes that modern Western art "has a tremendous philosophical and moral importance, because it represents, for the first time, a deliberate declaration by man of his will to master the world, to create it in conformity with his own ideals."[139]

Wilson felt the same. Art is consolation, an expression of faith in life. Paradoxically he sounds like Arnold or Keble, who speak of poetry as the *vis medica,* the healing power in a time of unbelief.

I have tried to show that Wilson cannot be simply dismissed as lacking a coherent point of view. He early adopted a version of Taine's determinism, and when he was converted to Marxism he assimilated the Marxist approach, deprived of its dialectic, to a general historical view of literature and literary study. Marxism became a variety of genetic explanations alongside psychoanalysis. Judicial criticism, the decision of what is good and what is bad in art, remained reserved to a judgment of taste independent of history.

I am aware that Wilson cannot be judged merely a theorist. On many questions he has nothing to say, for he has not thought them worthy of his attention. He is, and never claimed otherwise, a practical critic who has fulfilled his aims in reporting and judging books and authors from many countries on an enormous variety of subjects. He has opened windows, and not only to Russia. His human sympathy is almost unlimited. It extends, as he justly remarked, "even to those [manifestations of the American literary movement] of which, artistically, he disapproves,"[140] because he wanted to assert the dignity of the literary vocation in America. This sympathy seems, on occasion, too indiscriminate when we think of his weakness for such trivial authors as Ronald Firbank or shallow *raconteurs* such as Casanova, whom Wilson prefers to Rousseau,[141] or for eccentrics such as J. J. Chapman. Still, we might find his hero-worship for teachers such as Mr. Rolfe or Dean Gauss touching, and I for one make no complaints about his contempt for detective fiction and historical romances.

Still, there are definite limits to the reach of his mind. I am not thinking only of his obvious lack of technical skill in analyzing narrative modes or poetic structures. More disturbing is the coarseness and even vulgarity of his dominant interest in sex, displayed in some of the fiction and, obsessively, in the early notebooks. He shows hardly any interest in the fine arts or music. He lacks understanding not only for religion, which he treats as a "delusion," but also for philosophy. The early enthusiasm for Whitehead, his "crystalline abstract thought,"[142] seems to be based on a misunderstanding. It supported Wilson in his limited sympathies for symbolism and made him discount the "two divisions of mind and matter, body and soul,"[143] also in his polemics against the Neohumanists.

But Wilson could not share Whitehead's neoplatonic idealism or his concept of God, and Wilson soon abandoned Whitehead for Marxism. But as Wilson's Marxism discarded the dialectic, it meant rather a return to a basic positivism and pragmatism, a commonsense attitude to reality.

One sees this also in the comment on existentialism, which Wilson ridiculed for its assumption that "the predicament of the patriotic Frenchmen oppressed by the German occupation represents the condition of all mankind."[144] Wilson seems not to know that existentialism goes back to Heidegger and ultimately to Kierkegaard. Wilson thus could not escape from the limitations of a world view fundamentally akin to his early masters, Bernard Shaw and H. G. Wells, however much he transcended their provincialism. In spite of his cosmopolitism, his wide range of interests, there is a closeness and even crudity about his self-assurance and air of authority. But as public critic he dominates the early twentieth century with a resonance unmatched by any of the New Critics.

Notes

1. Henry Brandon, "We Don't Know Where We Are," a conversation with Edmund Wilson in *New Republic* 140(March 30, 1959), pp. 13–14.

2. Edmund Wilson, *The Shock of Recognition* 2nd ed. (New York: Farrar, Straus, and Co., 1955), Foreword.

3. Both in Edmund Wilson, *The Triple Thinkers* (New York: Harcourt, Brace, and Co., 1938), pp. 197, 212, 257–70.

4. Leon Edel, ed., *The Twenties: From Notebooks and Diaries of the Period* (New York: Farrar, Straus, and Giroux, 1975), p. 426.

5. Edmund Wilson, *Classics and Commercials* (New York: Farrar, Straus, and Co., 1950), p. 518.

6. Edmund Wilson, *The Shores of Light* (New York: Farrar, Straus, and Co., 1952), p. 546.

7. Edmund Wilson, *The Bit Between My Teeth* (New York: Farrar, Straus, and Giroux, 1965), pp. 535–36.

8. Ibid., p. 546.

9. Ibid., p. 553.

10. Ibid., p. 576.

11. Ibid., p. 553; almost identical reference on p. 381.

12. Edmund Wilson, "Uncle Matthew," *New Republic* 98 (22 March 1939): 199–200.

13. *Shores of Light*, p. 436.

14. Edmund Wilson, *Axel's Castle* (New York: Charles Scribner's Sons, 1931), pp. 115, 116–17.

15. *Shores of Light*, pp. 713–14.

16. *Axel's Castle*, p. 124.

17. Ibid., p. 122.

18. *Bit Between My Teeth*, pp. 372–73.

19. Ibid., pp. 384–86.

20. *Shores of Light*, pp. 451–67, 468–75. See also Johann Peter Eckermann, *Gespräche mit Goethe*, 28 March 1827, ed. H. H. Houben (Leipzig: 1948), p. 480.

21. *Shores of Light*, pp. 460, 463, 466.

22. *Bit Between My Teeth*, pp. 384, 397, 535.

23. *Triple Thinkers*, pp. 3–14.

24. Edmund Wilson, *The Devils and Canon Barham* (New York: Farrar, Straus, and Giroux, 1973), p. 92.

25. Leonard Kriegel, *Edmund Wilson* (Carbondale, Ill.: Southern Illinois University Press, 1971), p. 9.

26. *Bit Between My Teeth*, p. 30.

27. *Shores of Light*, p. 296; *Bit Between My Teeth*, pp. 32, 33; *Shores of Light*, p. 159; *The Devils*, p. 104.

28. *Shores of Light*, p. 143.

29. Ibid., p. 164.

30. *Bit Between My Teeth*, pp. 554–55.

31. *Classics and Commercials*, pp. 13, 15.

32. Ibid., p. 227.

33. Ibid., pp. 10–11.

34. See "Mr. Rolfe" in *Triple Thinkers*, pp. 233–56.

35. Edmund Wilson, *A Prelude* (New York: Farrar, Straus, and Giroux, 1967), p. 62.

36. *Shores of Light*, p. 36. *The Papers of Christian Gauss*, ed. Katherine Gauss Jackson and Hiram Haydn (New York: Random House, 1957), and his other published writings do not bear out his eminence as a critic and literary historian.

37. In Jackson and Haydn, *The Papers of Christian Gauss*.

38. Edmund Wilson, *The American Jitters* (Freeport, N.Y.: Books for Libraries Press, 1932; reprinted 1968), p. 307. This chapter was dropped from the reprint in his *The American Earthquake* (Garden City, N.Y.: Doubleday, 1958). A similar passage is in his *A Prelude*, p. 227.

39. *A Prelude*, p. 268.

40. *Shores of Light*, p. 229.

41. Edmund Wilson, *Red, Black, Blond, and Olive* (New York: Oxford University Press, 1956), p. 375.

42. Edmund Wilson, *To the Finland Station* (Garden City, N.Y.: Anchor Books, 1953), p. 452.

43. *The Twenties*, p. 245; a letter to Allen Tate dated 1928.

44. Edmund Wilson, *A Piece of My Mind* (Garden City, N.Y.: Anchor Books, 1958), pp. 59, 232.

45. See also Richard David Ramsey, comp., *Edmund Wilson: A Bibliography* (New York: D. Lewis, 1971).

46. *Bit Between My Teeth*, p. 2.

47. *Finland Station*, pp. 44–45, 49; compare with *Triple Thinkers*, pp. 260–61.

48. *Classics and Commercials*, p. 333.

49. *Finland Station*, pp. 306–307.

50. *Classics and Commercials*, pp. 487, 492.

51. *Shores of Light*, pp. 346–47.

52. Ibid., p. 749.

53. *Red, Black, Blond, and Olive*, pp. 413–18.

54. *Classics and Commercials*, p. 172.

55. *Bit Between My Teeth*, p. 146.

56. *Classics and Commercials*, p. 439. Beerbohm belongs to the "cultivated merchant class." See *Triple Thinkers*, p. 224, on Jonson's background.

57. *The Devil*, p. 59ff.

58. Edmund Wilson, *Patriotic Gore* (New York: Oxford University Press, 1962), p. 35. See also Wilson's notes on Arthur Schlesinger, Jr.

59. *Classics and Commercials*, pp. 169–70.

60. *Axel's Castle*, pp. 3, 5.

61. Edmund Wilson, "Modern Literature: Between the Whirlpool and the Rocky," *New Republic* 48 (2 November 1926): 296–97.

62. Emeric Fiser, *L'Esthétique de Marcel Proust* (Paris, 1933), Preface.

63. *Axel's Castle*, pp. 158, 221–22.

64. Ibid., p. 79.

65. Ibid., pp. 164, 218–19, 283.

66. Edmund Wilson, "A Preface to Modern Literature," *New Republic* 58 (20 March 1929): 134–35, and Edmund Wilson, "Axël and Rimbaud," *New Republic* 62 (26 February 1930): 34–40, concluded in Edmund Wilson, "Axël

and Rimbaud: III," *New Republic* 62 (5 March 1930): 69–73.

67. *Axel's Castle,* p. 245.

68. Ibid., pp. 263, 283.

69. Ibid., p. 293.

70. "The Literary Class War," 4 May 1932, in *Shores of Light,* p. 535.

71. *Triple Thinkers,* p. 77.

72. Ibid., p. 80.

73. Ibid., p. 199. Note that this passage comes from the "Einführung zur Kritikder politischen Ökonomie" (1857), a manuscript that was abandoned and was published in an obscure journal in 1903: *Die Neue Zeit* 21 (1903): 710–18, 741–45, 772–81.

74. *Triple Thinkers,* p. 204.

75. Ibid., pp. 205–207.

76. Ibid., pp. 208, 209, 212.

77. *The Twenties,* pp. 129, 421.

78. *Triple Thinkers,* pp. 262, 263, 265.

79. Ibid., pp. 266–67.

80. Ibid., pp. 267–70.

81. *Shores of Light,* p. 210.

82. *Triple Thinkers,* pp. 27–29.

83. *Classics and Commercials,* pp. 306, 368–69.

84. *Shores of Light,* p. 376.

85. *Bit Between My Teeth,* p. 47.

86. *Shores of Light,* p. 603.

87. *Bit Between My Teeth,* p. 5.

88. *Triple Thinkers,* pp. 254–55.

89. *Finland Station,* pp. 190, 194, 298.

90. Ibid., p. 436.

91. *Shores of Light,* p. 650.

92. Ibid., p. 501.

93. *Finland Station,* p. 187.

94. *Shores of Light,* p. 501.

95. Edmund Wilson, "Are Artists People?" *New Masses* 3 (January 1927): 5–9.

96. Edmund Wilson, "The Progress of Psychoanalysis: The Importance of the Discovery, by Dr. Sigmund Freud, of the Subconscious Self" *Vanity Fair* 14 (August 1920): 41, 86, 88.

97. *Axel's Castle,* p. 176.

98. Edmund Wilson, *The Wound and the Bow* (Boston: Houghton Mifflin, 1941), p. 294.

99. Ibid., pp. 287, 289.

100. Ibid., pp. 102–103.

101. A. E. Dyson, *The Inimitable Dickens* (New York: St. Martin's Press, 1970), rejects Wilson's view, but Angus Wilson accepts it, with some hesitation. (See Introduction to Penguin Edition of Charles Dickens *The Mystery of Edwin Drood* [1974], p. 23.)

102. *Wound and the Bow,* pp. 111, 114, 123.

103. Ibid., pp. 138, 143.

104. Ibid., p. 166.

105. *Triple Thinkers*, p. 88.

106. F. O. Matthiessen and K. Murdock, eds., *The Notebooks* (New York: Oxford University Press, 1947), pp. 178–79. I quote the refutation by F. R. Leavis in *Scrutiny* 18 (1950): 117. There is an incredibly inflated literature on this story.

107. *Triple Thinkers*, pp. 100–101.

108. Ibid., pp. 129, 130n.

109. Ibid., pp. 106, 111.

110. Edmund Wilson, "Henry James," *Nassau Literary Magazine* 70 (November 1914): 286–95.

111. *Shores of Light*, p. 220.

112. *Triple Thinkers*, p. 219.

113. *Classics and Commercials*, pp. 216–17.

114. *Triple Thinkers*, p. 221.

115. Ibid., pp. 266–67.

116. "Is Verse a Dying Technique?", in *Triple Thinkers*, pp. 15–30. Originally ·published as "The Canons of Poetry" in *The Atlantic Monthly* 153 (April 1934): 455–62.

117. *Axel's Castle*, p. 82.

118. Ibid., pp. 118–20; *Triple Thinkers*, pp. 16–18.

119. Ibid., pp. 26–28.

120. *Patriotic Gore*, p. 489.

121. *Shores of Light*, p. 240.

122. Ibid., pp. 49, 50, 53, 241.

123. Ibid., p. 669; *Bit Between My Teeth*, p. 362.

124. *Shores of Light*, p. 45.

125. *Axel's Castle*, pp. 39, 40, 47, 59.

126. Ibid., p. 105.

127. *The Twenties*, pp. 247–48.

128. *Wound and the Bow*, pp. 126–27.

129. *Triple Thinkers*, p. 180.

130. *Classics and Cammercials*, p. 448.

131. *Triple Thinkers*, p. 46.

132. *Shores of Light*, p. 271.

133. *Triple Thinkers*, p. 46.

134. *Classics and Commercials*, p. 44.

135. *Bit Between My Teeth*, p. 272.

136. *Shores of Light*, p. 62.

137. Edmund Wilson, "Meditations on Dostoevsky," *New Republic* 56 (24 October 1928): 274–76. Note that *The Twenties*, p. 312, reads: "All of literature gives a false view of life." In Edmund Wilson, *I Thought of Daisy* (New York: Farrar, Straus, and Giroux, 1967), pp. 174–76, the sentiments of the Dostoevsky article are repeated, sometimes verbatim.

138. *Classics and Commercials*, p. 392.

139. *Bit Between My Teeth*, pp. 137, 139.

140. *Shores of Light*, p. 229.

141. *Wound and the Bow*, p. 192. But Wilson wrote an introduction to the

Borzoi edition of Jean Jacques Rosseau's *Confessions* (New York: A. A. Knopf 1923), which sees its importance as "the first real romantic autobiography."

142. *The Twenties,* p. 290.

143. Professor Grosbeake in *I Thought of Daisy* expounds Whitehead in these terms (p. 226). Wilson defended Whitehead against P. E. More (see *Shores of Light,* p. 465).

144. *Classics and Commercials,* p. 399.

Bibliography

Berthoff, Werner. *Edmund Wilson.* University of Minnesota Pamphlets on American Writers. Number 67. Minneapolis, Minnesota: University of Minnesota Press, 1968.

Farrelly, John. In *Scrutiny* 18(1951–52): 229–33.

Frank, Charles P. *Edmund Wilson.* New York: Twayne Publ., 1970.

Gilman, Richard. "E. Wilson: Then and Now." *New Republic* 1955(2 July 1966): 23–28.

Heilman, Robert B. "The Freudian Reading of *The Turn of the Screw,*" Modern Language Notes 62(November 1947): 473–45.

Hyman, Stanley Edgar. In *The Armed Vision.* New York: A. A. Knopf, 1948, pp. 19–48.

Kazin, Alfred. In *Contemporaries.* Boston: Little, Brown. 1962, pp. 405–411.

———. *On Native Grounds.* New York: Reynal and Hitchcock, 1942, pp. 446–52.

———. *The Inmost Leaf.* New York: Harcourt, Brace and Co. 1955, pp. 93–97.

Kermode, Frank. In *Encounter* 26(May 1966): 61–66, 68, 70.

———. *In Puzzles and Epiphanies.* London: Routhedgeand K. Paul. 1962, pp. 55–63.

Kreigel, Leonard. *Edmund Wilson.* Carbondale, Ill.: Southern Illinois University Press, 1971.

Paul, Sherman. *Edmund Wilson: A Study of Literary Vocation in Our Time.* Urbana, Ill.: University of Illinois Press, 1965. Reprint 1966.

Podhoretz, Norman. In *Doings and Undoings.* London: R. Hart-Davis, 1964, pp. 30–50.

Ramsey, Richard David, comp. *Edmund Wilson: A Bibliography.* New York: D. Lewis, 1971.

Schwartz, Delmore. In *Selected Essays.* Chicago, Ill.: University of Chicago Press, pp. 360–74.

Wain, John. In *Essays on Literature and Ideas.* London: Macmillan, 1963, pp. 141–45.

Wilson, Edmund. *A Window on Russia.* New York: Farrar, Straus, and Giroux, 1972.

——. *Axel's Castle.* New York: Charles Scribner's Sons, 1931. Reprint 1945.

——. *Classics and Commercials.* New York: Farrar, Straus, and Co., 1950.

——. *Patriotic Gore.* New York: Oxford University Press, 1962.

——. *Red, Black, Blond, and Olive.* New York: Oxford University Press, 1956.

——. *The Bit Between My Teeth.* New York: Farrar, Straus, and Giroux, 1965.

——. *The Devils and Canon Barham.* New York: Farrar, Straus, and Giroux, 1972.

——. *The Shores of Light.* New York: Farrar, Straus, and Co., 1952.

——. *The Triple Thinkers.* New York: Harcourt, Brace, and Co., 1938. Revised and enlarged edition, New York: Oxford University Press, 1948. Reprint 1963.

——. *The Twenties: From Notebooks and Diaries of the Period.* Edited by Leon Edel. New York: Farrar, Straus, and Giroux, 1975.

——. *The Wound and the Bow.* Boston: Houghton Mifflin Co., 1941.

——. *To the Finland Station.* Garden City, N.Y.: Anchor Books, 1953.

Index

Engels, Friedrich, 70, 75, 77
Euthyphro, 32
Expression, vs. thought, 21–24
Expressiveness, and matching, in art, 9–10; vs. signification, 13–14

Fiedler, Leslie, 65
Firbank, Ronald, 71–72, 89
Fitzgerald, F. Scott, 67
Flaubert, Gustave, 68, 74–75
Forgery, in art, 45, 54, 57
Foster, William Z., 69
Frank, Charles P., 71
Frederic, Harold, 72
Freedom, and philosophy, 26, 32
Frege, Gottlob, 20, 22
Freud, Sigmund, 68, 83, 84
Frost, Robert, 85

Garrick, David, 42
Gauss, Christian, 69, 89
George, Stefan, 73
Getlein, Frank, 15
God, concept of, 27; works of, vs. works of art, 46
Goethe, Johann Wolfgang von, 66
Gogol, Nikolai, 83
Gold, Michael, 74
Gombrich, E. H., 9–15
Good Earth, The (Buck), 44, 51–52
Goodman, Nelson, 10

Hamsun, Knut, 44, 51–52
Handel, George Frederick, 57
Harries, Karsten, 46
Hegel, Georg Wilhelm Frederick, 77
Heidegger, Martin, 27, 28, 34, 89
Hemingway, Ernest, 76
Herder, Johan Gottfried, 45–46, 77
Hertz, Heinrich Rudolf, 20
Hicks, Granville, 76
Historicism, and literary criticism, 45–46
History, relevance to art criticism, 1–17, 55–58; and philosophy, 19–37; recording of, selective, 39–40; instant, not possible, 40; art criticism linked to, 42; literary, and literary criticism, 43–46, 47–50
Hölderlin, Johann Christian, 60–61

Homer, 79
Housman, A. E., 78
Hugo, Victor, 68
Humanism, 66–67, 79
Huneker, James, 68
Huxley, Aldous, 87
Huysmans, Joris Karl, 68
Hyman, Stanley, 71

Ibsen, Henrik, 68
Imitation, in literature, 44, 51–52
Interpretation, of poetry, 59–61

James, Henry, 65, 82–83
Johnson, Samuel, 66, 77
Jonson, Ben, 72, 83
Joyce, James, 66, 73–74, 83

Kafka, Franz, 88
Kandinsky, Wassily, 12–13
Kant, Immanuel, 20, 21, 22, 47
Kazin, Alfred, 71
Keats, John, 48–49, 59, 64
Keble, John, 88
Kermode, Frank, 71
Kierkegaard, Sören, 89
Kipling, Rudyard, 81–82
Kittredge, George Lyman, 49
Klee, Paul, 13
Kostelanetz, Richard, 53
Kriegel, Leonard, 71

Laches, 32
Language, and philosophy, 29–32
Larbaud, Valéry, 73
Lasalle, Ferdinand, 75
Leavis, F. R., 64, 83
Leibniz, Gottfried Wilhelm von, 45–46
Lenin, Nikolai, 70, 75
Levitine, George, 15
Literary criticism, and literary history, 43–46, 47–50; comparison in, 51–52; and Marxism, 74–77, 79–80; and psychoanalysis, 77, 80–84; and taste, 77–78; Edmund Wilson's views on, 78–79; evolution of Edmund Wilson's, 88–89
Literature, imitation in, 44, 51–52; elucidated by history, 43–44; understanding of, sometimes obscured by literary his-

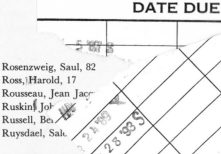